with

Are We There Yet

Is the Sun Setting on Planet Earth?

Joyce Hum

authorHOUSE

AuthorHouse™
1663 Liberty Drive
Bloomington, IN 47403
www.authorhouse.com
Phone: 1 (800) 839-8640

© 2020 Joyce Hum. All rights reserved.

No part of this book may be reproduced, stored in a retrieval system, or transmitted by any means without the written permission of the author.

Published by AuthorHouse   07/07/2020

ISBN: 978-1-7283-6623-4 (sc)
ISBN: 978-1-7283-6621-0 (hc)
ISBN: 978-1-7283-6622-7 (e)

Library of Congress Control Number: 2020912035

Print information available on the last page.

Cover Photograph: Angela Tyler – Used by permission.

Scripture quotations marked NIV are taken from the Holy Bible, New International Version®. NIV®. Copyright © 1973, 1978, 1984 by International Bible Society. Used by permission of Zondervan. All rights reserved. [Biblica]

This book is printed on acid-free paper.

Because of the dynamic nature of the Internet, any web addresses or links contained in this book may have changed since publication and may no longer be valid. The views expressed in this work are solely those of the author and do not necessarily reflect the views of the publisher, and the publisher hereby disclaims any responsibility for them.

Holy Bible – The New International Version

2 Peter 1: 19 – 21

> 19. We also have the prophetic message as something completely reliable, and you will do well to pay attention to it, as to a light shining in a dark place, until the day dawns and the morning star rises in your hearts. 20. Above all, you must understand that no prophecy of Scripture came about by the prophet's own interpretation of things. 21. For prophecy never had its origin in the human will, but prophets, though human, spoke from God as they were carried along by the Holy Spirit.

Preface

Knowing what the future holds is important. This question often intrigues us. Knowing for certain I was going to die tomorrow would definitely impact my decisions today. The truth of the matter is we do not know what tomorrow will bring. We have our assumptions, so we go from day to day based on the current predictable circumstances.

But what about the future? Many things concern us; pollution is everywhere. Poverty, and homelessness are major concerns. Excessive world debt is concerning. Will wise people come to our rescue?

Our environmental issues are considered so grave that some are asking if our planet will even survive. I am a Christian who believes in God. I also believe that I, along with all others, have a responsibility for protecting our planet.

We are mere specks in the universe. We live on this little green planet twirling around in a massive universe. Where are we going and to what end? Once upon a time there was no earth. But here we are and how did it all begin?

Many people have over the years pondered these questions. Great thinkers, researchers and philosophers have spent much time and money trying to figure this all out.

A special book out there asserts it has the answers to all our wonderment. This book is called the Holy Bible. It begins with an account of the creation of Earth, and ends with its destruction, followed by a new beginning.

The Bible tells us we too are God's creation, and that God loves us and wants the best for us. Each person is a wonderful creation. We are each given a free will and the right to choose. I believe each person has an important role to play. Our role is to figure out how to live our lives and how to treat others. The good news is that we are not alone. By God's grace we can seek him for guidance and wisdom.

The Bible needs to be read by all, because I believe it is the Word of God, written through men but given by God. With the invention of the Internet, the Bible is available to billions of people in many different languages, and many nations. Could this too, be part of God's plan?

God tells us about the future through Biblical prophecies. Biblical prophecy, gives us information on future happenings that will occur on Earth. Many Biblical prophecies have been fulfilled and others will come. God in his wisdom wants us to know what is yet to come.

This book, Are We There Yet? examines past and current events to ascertain where we might be on God's time line and to encourage us for the times ahead. Keeping in mind that God is working out His will on the earth, we can trust in His awesome power.

Currently, we face many unusual challenges, including a pandemic. The predictable is no longer our normal. What might our futures hold? I ask God to impart His truth and wisdom to me and to all readers as we learn together. For praise, honor and glory belong to Him.

Contents

Chapter 1 – What Can It Be?	1
Chapter 2 – A Historical View	5
Chapter 3 – Wealth Of Nations	8
Chapter 4 – The Power Of Knowing	13
Chapter 5 – The Meaning Of Time	18
Chapter 6 – Amassing Knowledge	22
Chapter 7 – Who We Are	27
Chapter 8 – Taking Charge	32
Chapter 9 – Jews, Gentiles And The Sabbath Rest	37
Chapter 10 – The Time Is Near	41
Chapter 11 – Deception	47
Chapter 12 – Pay Attention To Biblical Prophecies	51
Chapter 13 – Prophecies Of Daniel	54
Chapter 14 – The Revelation Of Jesus Christ	68
Chapter 15 – Claim Your Inheritance	90
Endnotes: Sources of Information	95
Annex A: Four Prophecies of Daniel	97
Annex B: Summary Of The Book Of Revelation	99

Chapter 1

What Can It Be?

Unpredictable World

The words that come to us often are "oh no, not again!" Bad news has become far too common. We want to hold on to our beliefs and expectations, these allow us to live our lives comfortably. However, this model may no longer be appropriate. Unpredictable leads to uncertainty, what can it be?

After many discussions and much research, I can safely say that there is an unsettling feeling out there that is affecting many, including me. Feelings are often difficult to explain but they are real. Many things have become more unpredictable. It is difficult to come up with substantial explanations. Could this be our new normal?

Storms have become larger and more frequent. When it rains, it pours and causes flooding. When the wind blows, tornadoes occur. Many countries are contending with uncontrollable fires. Our climate is changing and not for the better. Added to climate change we have many earthquakes and volcanoes that are playing havoc on Earth.

Murders, including shootings and stabbings are on the increase. Both adults and children are killing themselves and others. Violence is everywhere. People are dying on the streets of drug overdose. Homelessness, mental health issues, and poverty are far too common. There are millions of displaced people from many countries trying to escape suffering for themselves and their children.

Added to all this, a new Coronavirus, called Covid-19, emerged in China, and has spread to most countries. Professionals are working to find solutions for containment and an antivirus solution. Politicians and people from all over the world are very concerned. Many countries put their populations in lockdowns. Major cities in China, Italy, the United States, Canada, and other countries became quiet as people stayed in their homes or in hospitals.

Economically, the impact of Covid-19 is being felt on the world stage as job losses are huge and stock markets are affected. Many countries, including Canada and the United States, have economies that are built on accumulated debt. Coping with the unplanned health issue, is causing decreased economic activity that in turn is increasing economic uncertainty.

Climate Change

Global warming is getting world-wide attention and many believe it is the underlying cause of negative changes in our climate. Under the Paris Climate Accord, many countries came together in 2015, and agreed to decrease the amount of carbon emissions in our atmosphere. Carbon buildup in the atmosphere is seen as man-made, as much of it comes from our use of fossil fuels as a major source of energy.

In practical terms what does this mean? Will we see less air travel, will our fuel happy trucks and SUVs be set aside? Will we stop burning coal and diesel fuel? Will we or can we move quickly toward a world where fossil fuels will be no longer used or needed? There is much that can be done but changing our buying habits is not very popular.

I live in Canada where we have long winters. My home is efficiently heated with a natural gas pipeline that comes directly into my home and my home is but one of millions.

Most political leaders know people want comfort over change. It is not easy to make difficult choices, when change leads to uncertainty. Governments know they will face an increased possibility of losing the next election. Yet, the lingering problem of carbon emissions and buildup needs to be addressed as a world issue.

Climate change is seen as a contributor to out of control bush fires. Australia has experienced devastating fires. Thousands of hectares have burned, including buildings and wildlife. Ongoing calls for prayer on social media were common. The good news is that the rains did come. Many regions around the world including Europe, North and South America have all experienced severe fires.

Climate change is also seen as a possible cause for the many storms and floods that have occurred and are occurring in many countries. Rain amounts were more predictable, now we are getting a month's worth of rain in mere hours. Streets are turning into rivers and cleanup costs are soaring. Storm sewers are no longer adequate, and cities are scrambling to find solutions. A country that can attest to this is Iran. During 2019 and continuing into 2020 Iran has had devastating rain.

Added to the rain issue there is a concern over melting ice. There is an enormous amount of frozen water at the South and North poles and these areas are melting. Scientific reports tell us that drastic actions must be taken by every country or soon it will be too late. Destroying this earth would be an unbearable disaster. We have looked far and wide with strong telescopes and nothing like our earth can be found.

Are We There Yet?

One must ask where is all this leading us, is this sustainable? Will wise leaders come forward to save the day? What do we mean when we ask

"Are We There yet?" Is the end of our little green planet in sight? Will it be destroyed, blown up or contaminated to a point where it becomes uninhabitable? Elon Musk, an American entrepreneur, seems to think the time is near. He talks about moving people to Mars.

Could we be at the point of no return for our earth due to climate change? We also might want to ask ourselves if this is an issue that only an all-powerful God can solve?

Chapter 2

A Historical View

Our Inhumanity

Our history of war is terrifying. From the first book of the Holy Bible, Genesis, to now, people have been killing one another. The fight over control and power goes on both in the offensive and defensive. Over the years, wars have increased in size, powerful weapons and technology have made us very efficient at killing. The destruction of the whole earth is now possible.

The many wars bring out the truth of our broken humanity. We have shown our willingness to do what we are told to do. The civil war in the United States demonstrates how even within a country, killing one another is used to solve our differences.

World War One was fought between 1914 and 1918. World War Two followed. Such inhumanity seems incomprehensible, but these wars happened. World War Two, started in 1939 when Britain, France and Poland declared war on the invading Germans. Other countries, including Canada, followed. In 1941, the United States joined the war effort after an attacked by Japan.

During this war, the Germans murdered six million Jews; men, women, and children, a supposedly Christian Country in Europe. Many countries in Europe were occupied by the Germans as their leader Adolf Hitler convinced his people to follow him. Italy and Japan, joined the Germans. Deaths caused by this war were around 60 million. How can a world, populated by supposedly rational people, partake in such cruelty? **1.**

Other wars have since occurred – The United States, along with other nations, took on the role of protecting democracy from communism and dictators. Many Americans and others, have been killed for this cause. Korea, Vietnam, Afghanistan, and Iraq have taken many lives. The Americans have had a limited degree of victory; however, Communism and dictators live on.

The United Nations

The United Nations, an organization that replaced the League of Nations was established in 1945. It currently consists of 193 sovereign member countries. The UN's mandate has been admirable as it seeks to maintain global peace and good governance. The UN Security Council provides a forum for key nations to broker solutions to promote peace. They have experienced a measure of success in a complex and politically divided world. **2.**

Defence

In 1945, the countries that border the North Atlantic Ocean formed an alliance, the North Atlantic Treaty Organization, and use the acronym NATO. The main goal of the treaty is to defend one another. It includes the United States, most EU members, Britain, Canada, and Turkey. Over the years the NATO countries have come together in times of war as well as working together on peace keeping duties. While they try, they need to do better. Sustainability requires a financial commitment by each country. Their stated goal is to have each member country spend a specified amount of their GDP on defence. However, many countries have not maintained their commitment leaving much of the cost requirements to the United States. This puts the entire concept of NATO into question. **3.**

Possible Wars

Looking back through history leaves one with the understanding that war is always a definite possibility. Will another war occur that will be so terrible we will destroy ourselves or make our beautiful earth uninhabitable? Are we there yet?

What about a nuclear war? Many countries now have enough war power to destroy our planet. North Korea certainly makes one nervous when we see a young dictator constantly testing its arsenal of weapons. Both the United States and Russia have nuclear weapons ready to fire at any time. Are we at a point in time where nuclear war will destroy our earth?

Time of Peace

The truth is, even with all the ongoing violence and unstable countries, we are living in a time of relative world peace. There continues to be civil unrest in Syria, Yemen, and east Africa. Iran, a country that is little trusted, especially by Israel, has caused havoc by arming Syria and Lebanon. However, the fact remains that no world wars are being fought. Will there be a world war Three? There might be. Personally, I do not think any country would want war. With the weapons of destruction currently available, this would be a losing situation for all.

Current Status - Israel

Israel became a nation state in 1948, Israel's return displaced many Palestinians who saw the area as their homeland. This situation continues as the Palestinians want the area returned to them. Negotiations continue to be off and on, but mainly the Palestinians see the land as theirs and refuse to accept Israel as a nation.

Chapter 3

Wealth Of Nations

Political Unity

On the positive side of peace and unity we now have a united Europe, the European Union. War among European countries has a lengthy history. I wonder what Napoleon would say if he could see a united Europe.

The European Union (EU) is a political and economic union with an estimated population of about 500 million and around 26 member states. Britain, through a vote in Parliament, left the EU on January 31, 2020. Working out a new trading agreement with the EU is now a high priority for Britain.

The EU has a developed market system and a standardised system of laws. They have free movement of people, goods, services for all members. According to my research, it has a GDP of around 19 trillion US dollars, approximately 25 % of the global economy. **4.**

As of November 2019, China's population stands around 1.4 billion. China, the world's most populated country, remains under a Communist regime but has embraced capitalism. It now has a large and growing middle-class. Likewise, India, which is a democracy, has a population of approximately 1.3 billion. It is also growing economically and building its middle-class. **5.**

The United States, Canada and Mexico, this year, 2020, passed a new free trade agreement. Canada now has a free trade deal with the EU. The United States and China appear to be experimenting with tariff wars that hopefully will eventually lead to an acceptable fair-trade deal with one another.

The global economy appears to be building a success story. According to the World Bank, in 1981, 42.3 percent of the population were living in extreme poverty; in 2015, that dropped to 10 percent. **6.**

The threat of Covid-19 to national economies is very real. Many businesses have had to close their doors. This is causing unemployment, and disrupting global supply chains making it difficult for businesses to even secure parts. National governments including Canada and the United States have taken measures to help the unemployed and extend temporary support to businesses. It is uncertain when vaccines will be available to treat Covid-19 but countries are hoping to quickly restart their economies when the threat of the virus diminishes.

Lasting Prosperity

Will world peace and our current level of economic wealth lead to lasting prosperity? Who could have imagined a united Europe, a united Europe brought about through peaceful negotiations that lead to acceptable treaties and increased wealth?

Negotiated trade treaties between and among nations that lead to increase globalization have also become a reality. These allow gains from trade that help our economies prosper. However, they also lead to greater dependence on one another. When one suffers, we will all suffer. Will we and can we learn from these concepts of cooperation and build on them to bring about lasting harmony, world peace and economic prosperity for all?

Looking deeper, one can see that much of what appears to be an economic success story for many, does not address serious issues and the needs of all. In the following words of Jesus, we begin to understand the importance he places on caring for everyone.

Matthew 25:40 – 46 (NIV)

> 40. "The King will reply, 'Truly I tell you, whatever you did for one of the least of these brothers and sisters of mine, you did for me.'
> 41. "Then he will say to those on his left, 'Depart from me, you who are cursed, into the eternal fire prepared for the devil and his angels.
> 42. For I was hungry and you gave me nothing to eat, I was thirsty and you gave me nothing to drink,
> 43. I was a stranger and you did not invite me in, I needed clothes and you did not clothe me, I was sick and in prison and you did not look after me.'
> 44. "They also will answer, 'Lord, when did we see you hungry or thirsty or a stranger or needing clothes or sick or in prison, and did not help you?'
> 45. "He will reply, 'Truly I tell you, whatever you did not do for one of the least of these, you did not do for me.'
> 46. "Then they will go away to eternal punishment, but the righteous to eternal life."

Missing the Mark

There is an expression in our societies that refers to plans that are being built on a house of cards. A house of cards is not a good thing in that it can easily fall apart. Once the house of cards falls apart it is not worth fixing. Mainly because you are again building a house of cards. Could it be that many countries are building themselves on a house of cards in that we have difficulty in caring for all?

The United States currently is the monetary reserve system of the world. The US economy as we know it is not sustainable due to spiralling debt and tax policies that favor corporate America. What is the country doing to address the needs of suffering people? The problems of the homeless, the under educated, the poor and working poor are not being addressed. In addition, inadequate health care and short-sighted migration policies continue to weaken and divide the country.

All this matters to people everywhere because should the United States lose its global monetary position, it will cause economic hardship for most nations.

I write these words in 2020; it is an election year in the U.S. The opportunity to elect a new president will be possible. Unfortunately, should a Democratic leader replace the current Republican leader would make little difference. Listening to both platforms leads to one conclusion. It does not matter who will lead America because many important issues will not be addressed. Power lies where power lies and the concern is mainly for those who vote.

Canada, the country in which I reside, depends heavily on the United States for its wealth and consequently is impacted by its policies. Canada, at all levels of government, federal, provincial, and municipal, is also deep in debt. Our next generation, our graduating students, are loaded with debt. If that is not enough, household debt is so high that international agencies are stating it as a risk factor. As in the United States, important issues regarding homelessness, people dying on the streets from drug overdosing and other suffering people are not sufficiently being addressed.

Will we be able to address these profound issues? I believe these issues are central to a Loving Holy God. I personally do not believe any political party in Canada will take these issues seriously enough to develop successful policies. Might the Canadian economy, like the United States, be another house of cards.

Possible Outcomes

Does this mean that the United States, Canada and other countries are reaching the point of no return in terms of policy development that keeps our nations strong and free? Are we going to move into a state of unrest where people are protesting and fighting in our streets? My observations lead me to say, maybe. I pray that somehow, we do not go down this path, but instead grab hold of policies that provides for all as well as doing our part for the environment. Should we allow our past to define our future? Things look bleak.

The lack of economic provision to many, and as I write this in 2020, the Covid-19 pandemic, are both causing human suffering. Could the outcome of the pandemic bring more despair or could it be an opportunity to consider changes that would be more inclusive? It should certainly be something to consider

Chapter 4

The Power Of Knowing

Important Questions

Governments around the world are too short sighted to protect the well being of their citizens. They strive to maintain power and avoid facing difficult choices. Will global warming be addressed or will our Earth become uninhabitable? Are we headed towards social unrest because our economic policies do not provide for the least of us? What can individuals do to face the future and deal with uncertainty?

Sharing Life's Journey

As I write these words and think about the many diverse issues we currently face, I am moved to share these experiences from my past. My hope is to bring to the reader, the understanding of the power and the importance of God. I go back to a time when life was good. I was studying at Carleton University in Ottawa, Canada.

Life was good not because I did not have problems, but because I had hope. The process of learning gave me an inner joy and a feeling of changing. Believing that if I were fortunate enough to graduate, I would get a job and have an outcome of independence and happiness for me and my children. I was the mother of four, ranging in age from six to ten.

I had been a believer in God, but I lived under fear with the constant threat of domestic violence. After spending much time in prayers of desperation, nothing changed and the violence continued. Accordingly, one day I made a heartfelt decision. I no longer would believe in God or continue with church.

Strangely, after this, things began to change. My neighbour told me I could take a course as a special student at Carleton University. I graduated four years later with a BA with a double major in Economics and Psychology. Due to my studies in Economics, I became employed with the federal government and finally, I was able to escape from my world of domestic violence.

At my place of employment there was a beautiful young lady named Cathy. Cathy would ask if I would like to attend a work-place Bible study. My answer was no. I had no interest whatsoever of having anything to do with the idea of God. One day, I was lonely and decided to go with her. Cathy gave me a Bible, a New Testament. I never had a Bible, nor had I read one.

Over time, I opened the Book and started reading it. A most unusual thing happened. Suddenly, words came to me that were not my own. "This is my Holy Word; I want you to read it and trust in it." My atheist heart did not know what to do. I continued going to the Bible study and cautiously continued reading the Bible. As I read, feelings of trust and love would come to me. I decided I would believe in God. The idea of Jesus I rejected. I reasoned that if the Jews rejected Jesus why would I not do the same.

As I read the Bible, its truths started coming to me. I soon realized that we, as humans, all sin. We have a sin nature within us. This gave me the understanding of the need for a Savior, and that Savior is Jesus Christ. God is a Holy God. In his domain, all sin must be paid for. Jesus Christ came to earth to become a divine sacrifice, acceptable to God. Through His cruel death on a cross, He paid for all sin. He defeated death by coming to life again and ascending into the clouds and now sits at the right hand of God his Father. After receiving this understanding, I confessed my belief in Jesus Christ as my Savior. I became what the Bible calls being born again, this time by the Spirit of God.

Continued Progress

This happened many years ago. I am now retired, and I call myself a Christian Outreach Worker. Over the years, for the most part, my life has been fruitful and successful.

I met and married Jamie, together we have faith and love for Jesus. We added to our family a beautiful daughter. Our main goal in life has been to do the work we feel called to do. Recently, the Spirit moved me to write this book, Are We There Yet? Jamie helps as my main critic, editor, and encourager.

My Christian growth has been and continues to be progressive through Bible reading and study, taking courses and attending a Bible believing church. Life's journey comes with surprises and understanding oneself is one of them. Learning one's weaknesses and our desperate need for improvement is all part of the process.

My difficult past had pushed me into wanting to live a life apart from God. However, along my path, a gracious God opened the door for me to understand my need for Him. He opened my understanding to see Him and the real me.

Important Knowledge

A very important message on God's love and very relevant to this discussion is found in the following Scripture.

2 Peter 3:8,9 (NIV)

> 8. But do not forget this one thing, dear friends: With the Lord a day is like a thousand years, and a thousand years are like a day.
> 9. The Lord is not slow in keeping his promise, as some understand slowness. Instead he is patient with you, not wanting anyone to perish, but everyone to come to repentance.

God wants no one to perish. He wants everyone to come to Him. Our sinful state keeps us separated from God, but we don't have to remain separated from God. I believe each person is loved by God. There is nothing we can do that will take God's love from us. He loves us even with our sin.

Jesus' sacrifice on the cross was costly. It was the will of God, our Heavenly Father, that all our terrible sin be paid for by the precious Blood of Jesus Christ. I pray daily that many hearts will be softened to recognize this important truth.

Our Earth is important to us and it is also important to God. He created it to be inhabited by many things, including people. From the simple flower growing along a deserted road to the oceans and all they contain; they are all His creation. He brings the rain and the sunshine that allows our food to grow. God's knowledge and power does it all. If we realized and understood our utter dependence upon a Holy God, we would be shaking in our boots.

Not a day passes that is not seen by God. My faith tells me that God sees things from an eternal perspective. He wants us to be with him for an eternity so how does this all fit into today's perspective. We are very near sighted and rarely do we understand the real meaning of things. An example of this in my life was a decision to obtain a major in economics. This decision brought me a changed life. Employment with the federal government, making a new friend who convinced me to go to a Bible study, meeting Jamie who became my husband and our daughter, are all a result of this decision. I thank God very often for leading me to study economics. I am so thankful. A merciful God led me even when I had little hope for a future.

God is all powerful. He is involved in individual lives as well as the Earth and the universe. We might think that we have to save our planet, but the truth is that the all-powerful God has a predetermined plan for His earth. Like it or not, we are all on God's time line. This time line will come to an end.

God is God and he is ultimately in control of his creation, including the Earth. I do not believe that God's Earth will be destroyed through the careless acts of people. I do however, believe that it is important to respect every created thing and accordingly, do our part in caring for God's beautiful Earth. God's timing and purpose is his alone. The concept of time is discussed further in the following chapter.

Chapter 5

The Meaning Of Time

The Concept

Thinking about time is usually seen as a measurement of movement. It takes approximately 365 days for the earth to circle the sun. Our year is divided into 365 days, days are divided into 24 hours, and hours into 60 minutes. One day leads to the next day and so on. Time is a passing commodity seen by us in moments of time that move consistently forward. Once gone it's gone.

The Holy Bible tells us that God, the creator of the universe sits on a throne in another dimension called Heaven. God and His divine Son Jesus Christ, are the creators of everything, including time. Referring to 2 Peter 8, 9 we see for God the concept of time is different than ours. A thousand years is like a day and a day is like a thousand years. In other words, God's concept of time is eternity. My mind has trouble with this perspective as I can only imagine a world where events come and go on a concept that we have a past and a future. However, I do believe eternity is real.

The Purpose of Time

God created time for a special purpose. I believe that purpose is you and me. Could it be that the time we experience here is our opportunity to make a choice that profoundly shapes our existence or lack thereof? Will intelligent beings who are free to choose, want to obey and trust in an unseen God? Having this right puts the responsibility on people to decide. Personally, I have to ask God often for his forgiveness, and for help to overcome my issues. Many decisions are required each day. We often make these decisions based on incorrect assumptions and wrong motives. The power of selfishness, pride and fear can easily set our paths. Realizing that Jesus Christ wants to be our guide makes for better decision making. I am exceedingly thankful that I can ask for his help and guidance every day to help me make the most of my God given time.

Evil Powers

Our journey "in time" on Earth is complex. Many are unaware that there are unseen evil powers. These powers come from Satan, and his demons who are enemies of God. While this is true, God is still in control. Should he decide to do so, all evil powers could be taken away in a blink of an eye. Instead, they are allowed to roam the earth. However, in God's timing they will be taken away.

In Revelation 12, we are told the story of Satan. An angel created by God became very prideful and wanted to replace God. A war was fought in Heaven. Michael, a warrior angel, defeated Satan and made him leave Heaven and come to earth. We are told that one third of the angels chose to follow Satan and are on earth with him. These angels who followed Satan are called demons. The Gospels, the first four books of the New Testament, tells of many events where Jesus delivered people from demons. These events show us the existence of demons and their power over people.

There continues to this day on Earth an ongoing war between angels who serve God and demons who serve Satan. They are unseen by humans, but very real. The demons work to keep people from knowing the truth about God and our Lord Jesus Christ.

Time belongs to God, and it will continue until God's appointed end. But because of our fallen nature and the impact of Satan, we will always have sin and the fallout from sin. Unfortunately, this is everyone's lot in life, and our only hope is Jesus.

The Impact of Evil

In the beginning of time everything was good. The first people created by God were placed in a beautiful place called Paradise in the Garden of Eden. They were told not to eat the fruit of one tree. This fruit contained the knowledge of good and evil. Satan came and tempted them through lies. They believed Satan and ate the fruit. This was a sin of pride and disobedience. The impact of sin was immediate.

Adam and Eve were removed from the Garden of Eden. Cain, Adam's son killed his brother Abel. Along with sin came sickness, physical death, violence, lies, greed and much pride as we try and be our own god. As stated earlier, sin is in our nature and it follows all generations.

The Need for Time

Time started with creation and it will continue on God's time line until it is no longer needed by God. For each person, time starts with conception, we develop in the womb until birth and live our lives until physical death occurs. Psalm 90:10 says that our lives may come to seventy years or eighty if our strength endures. Our bodies stay on the Earth but our spirits go upward, those whose name is written in the Lamb's Book of Life go to Heaven, while others are separated from God.

God's Goal

God has never stopped being involved in the lives of people. His main goal is to have a relationship with people as Father. People, during their earthly time can be reconciled back to God the Father, through their belief in Jesus. I can safely say that God's actions, no matter if we understand them or not, are always based on the concept of eternity and his love for us, wanting to be our heavenly Father.

A Way Forward

Our beginning was darkened with man's fall into sin. However, God established a plan to again have people come into relationship with him. He provided a way forward for people to be reconciled back to himself through his divine Son.

This began when God called a man named Abram, who became Abraham. He wanted a people who would demonstrate his character to broken humanity and overtime lead to a Savior. God told Abraham that all generations would be blessed through him. This was accomplished through his descendants leading to King David, and from King David's lineage to Jesus. The genealogy of Jesus can be found in Matthew 1.

Our Struggle Continues

We are told that most find it difficult to follow God.

Matthew 7:13, 14, (NIV)

> 13. Enter through the narrow gate. For wide is the gate and broad is the road that leads to destruction, and many enter through it. 14. But small is the gate and narrow the road that leads to life, and only a few find it.

Is our use of time important? From God's perspective, it is probably our most precious gift. Hence, we must use our time with care. I believe that God wants none to be lost on the road that leads to destruction. He loves each person and his most important goal is to be our Heavenly Father and have us with him and with Jesus for an eternity.

Chapter 6

Amassing Knowledge

Use of Knowledge

When I ponder our history, I am confounded. Our world, this Earth and its inhabitants, have survived much. When I consider all the wars over the years, it is amazing that we continue at all. The suffering caused by war is immeasurable. It breaks my heart to see the many people fleeing their homelands, desperately trying to find some level of peace and safety for themselves and their families. Compassion is paramount when people are hurting but often it appears to be missing. Knowledge that people are suffering does not necessarily bring those in leadership to help them, even in one's own country. Syria is a very sad example of this.

Acquiring more knowledge doesn't seem to be correlated with better behavior. In other words, we know better but often behavior does not reflect knowledge. Brothers and sisters fight among themselves. Husbands and wives often cannot work out their differences. White people say mean things about brown people, and brown people say mean things about white people. Everybody likes to criticize those in authority no matter what they do or how hard they try.

Are we unable to change, or is this just who we are? This leads me to think about our broken humanity. I really do find it amazing that we still exist. Could it be that we continue not because of us but in spite of us?

While we have many weaknesses, I also see that people have the capacity to overcome and accomplish astonishing things. We learn, we apply our learning to our world, and consequently, we have moved forward over the years building upon the knowledge and progress of past generations. For this I say good for us.

Technologies

New technologies are a great example of our progress. Over the years, many useful conveniences and advancements in science have come out of our discoveries. Technology is used in amazing ways and keeps advancing every day. Our accumulated knowledge on the use of electricity has changed every facet of our daily lives. Air transportation now allows us to travel the world.

Our current technologies assist us to do complicated endeavors that for the average person is impossible to comprehend. The hand-held computer, what we call the smart-phone is an example of our progress. Facebook, Instagram, and other platforms allow one to send messages, see one another in real time and post information to anywhere in the world. We call this social media and because of paid advertisements, much of it is free to all who have access to the internet.

Agriculture

We now have over seven billion people living on Earth. A number that is incomprehensible to me. How in the world do we manage to feed, clothe and house all these people? How can we do this? Over the years many have forecast that our population would become so large that feeding them would be impossible. However, even with seven billion people we manage to produce food surpluses.

Our agriculture techniques have evolved where not only is there enough food for all, but over the years, fewer and fewer people are employed in its production. This is not to say that we have no hungry people. The lack is not because of shortages, but is one of faulty distribution, usually a result of unstable governance and dysfunctional and outdated practices and laws.

In Canada, when we walk into our grocery stores and markets, we see heaps of produce, meats and other things. We are a rich country. Unfortunately, there are people throughout our land who have problems of affordable housing, unemployment or illnesses, which make it difficult for them. We have government programs, both federal and provincial that help. We also have private organizations such as the Salvation Army, food banks and many other charities who work tirelessly to provide for those in need.

God's Provision

Where does God, the creator of everything fit into this need? Does knowledge come from God, and is it part of His provision? Almost everything we eat is living and everything growing requires water. God is the sender of the rain.

Matthew 5:45 (NIV)

> 45. ….He causes his sun to rise on the evil and the good, and sends rain on the righteous and the unrighteous.

Acts 14:17 (NIV)

> 17. Yet he has not left Himself without testimony: He has shown kindness by giving you rain from heaven and crops in their seasons; he provides you with plenty of food and fills your hearts with joy.

Did we invent carrots, corn or rice? Are these not all living things we have at the good pleasure of God? Do we appreciate how dependent we are on the God who created everything? Our dependence upon God is our life. Whether we acknowledge or reject our dependence does not change this important truth.

How does the God of the universe fit into our understanding and knowledge? Could it be most of our knowledge comes from an all knowing and merciful God? The Book of Isaiah in the Old Testament tells us where our knowledge comes from. In Chapter 28, verses 23 to 29, we are given a descriptive narrative about a farmer who wants to grow different types of grain:

> 23. Listen and hear my voice; pay attention and hear what I say.
> 24. When a farmer plows for planting, does he plow continually? Does he keep on breaking up and working the soil?
> 25. When he has leveled the surface, does he not sow caraway and scatter cumin? Does he not plant wheat in its place, barley in its plot, and spelt in its field?
> 26. His God instructs him and teaches him the right way.
> 27. Caraway is not threshed with a sledge, nor is the wheel of a cart rolled over cumin; caraway is beaten out with a rod, and cumin with a stick.
> 28. Grain must be ground to make bread; so one does not go on threshing it forever. The wheels of a threshing cart may be rolled over it, but one does not use horses to grind grain.
> 29. All this also comes from the Lord Almighty, whose plan is wonderful, whose wisdom is magnificent.

I believe that God gives us knowledge in every area to help us have a better life here on Earth, and this includes our use of new technologies.

I recently listened to a documentary about a person in England, George Boole, who in 1854 developed the mathematics that form the basis of our computer language and the internet. This was picked up and used many years later by others. Could God have imparted this knowledge to George Boole? Again, perhaps we are far more dependent on God for our knowledge than we would like to admit.

Could it be that all our knowledge comes from God? Our use of electricity is essential to much of our progress. Did we create electricity or have we merely been given knowledge on how to use it? I believe that God gives us knowledge and intelligence for understanding that allows us to live better and more productive lives.

God knows and understands everything. We as created beings with limitations are very blessed to have an all-knowing God share important truths with us. This truth should aid us to be humble and thankful for every progress made and continue to ask him to reveal even more to us. As mentioned earlier, many are being impacted negatively by the Covid-19 virus. My approach to this is to be humble and ask our all-knowing Heavenly Father to show us how to master this and move forward with living.

Chapter 7

Who We Are

Our Nature

Much can be learned by looking backwards. What does history tell us about the nature of people? Many wars have been fought. People are often discriminated against and even killed for being who they were meant to be. People murder others, and we see brothers who fight against their brothers. Families are often in disarray as spouses cannot solve their disagreements.

The first thing that comes to mind is that each person, yes, each of us, is terribly broken. We all are born with a sin nature. I believe it might be easier for us to live a life of sin than a life of doing good, as we are all inherently selfish. People want to be their own god. Wanting to control one's life and others is an outward expression of this.

Since the beginning of people, our history has been one of sin and violence. God programmed the animals but not people. He gave humans a free will. Why did Adam and Eve eat the apple that God told them not to eat? God granted both Adam and Eve the right to choose.

The Good

While the above is true, there is also another side. We are very important to God and highly valued. We are so valued, that I believe this Earth and everything on it was made for you and for me. We are all God's prized possession. We are important to God and we are loved by God. He also wants us to value ourselves. The Bible tells us that nothing can separate us from the love of God.

We are each wonderfully made, body, mind and spirit. We are miracles of creation. Our bodies are so complex that researchers and the medical profession have been trying to figure it out for years. Our mind thinks and makes sense of our world for us. Our inner spirit is constantly growing and changing. We are without a doubt, amazing.

Never allow yourself to question your worth. Many people take their own lives due to despair. Your life matters. It matters to God, your family, your friends and even to those whom you don't know. When a life is stopped, it takes away all the subsequent possibilities that were meant to be.

Selfishness

Our selfishness comes from the need to survive and who can blame us, surviving in our world is an important objective. Will we share our wealth and time with others or will we want to attain and keep our wealth for ourselves and our families? Do we demand government policies that give us a better life at the expense of others? The truth is, our futures are often diminished due to our short sightedness, our selfishness and our need for survival. Our vision would be less short sighted, if we would take into consideration and learn about the power of a loving and caring God.

In Luke, chapter 10, Jesus answers the question who is our neighbor by giving us a story about the reaction of a good Samaritan. The Samaritan sees a beaten and wounded person lying on the ground. He stops and helps the person. He takes him to an Inn and pays the Inn Keeper to provide care for the beaten man. Jesus contrasts this behavior with a priest who moves to the other side of the street and does nothing to help the wounded person. What would you do? Probably, most of us would be like the priest. Personally, I would call 911 and have the person cared for but little else. Jesus gave us this example so we can see our shortcomings.

True Success

I am no different than my fellow man. You probably are no different than your fellow man. We all come with many weaknesses. One folly that often causes much stress is how we define and measure success. Often, this happens so subtly that one rarely questions it. We believe that to "succeed" in life we must somehow do better than our neighbor. This leads us to a future of competitiveness and stress.

Is it even possible to overcome this? We learn much of what we do and think from others. However, our time on earth is ours individually. We have families, friends and acquaintances, but the bottom line is that we are individuals. Each person is accountable for their decisions.

Others Who Influence

In our lives we have both positive and negative experiences that affect us. We often blame our families for our unhappy feelings, but there are many other influences that shape who we are. Most people find themselves suffering from things that wounded their inner being. Always understand that God sees all our history and wants to be included in our healing process. Accordingly, talk to God about your pain, asking Him for relief and inner healing. One can share and pray with a trusted friend. A prayer that has been helpful to me is to ask Jesus to help me rise above my past and bring healing into my heart. Praying with determination is key. Jesus does not want us to live out our time suffering and wounded.

Jesus said that if we follow him, we will receive a peace that passes all understanding. This promise does not come easily. I have achieved a measure of peace as I strive to trust my Savior Jesus Christ more and more each day.

We are All Equal

Jesus teaches us that we are all equal and highly valued. We often think of ourselves and the world in terms of our occupations, our wealth or lack thereof, and our education as we compare ourselves with others. The important thing is how does God see us. In my past, I wasted much time "wanting to be someone". My biggest problem was my definition of "someone". I am certain my definition and God's, were miles apart. The question that needs asking is "Lord, is this what you want for my life?" God always see us differently than we see ourselves. We are already "someone" to God. To be overly concerned with most of the stuff that bothers us, might be a waste of our precious time that God has given us.

Galatians 3: 28 (NIV)

> There is neither Jew nor Gentile, neither slave nor free, nor is there male and female, for you are all one in Christ Jesus.

This Scripture tells us each and every one of us has value, in the eyes of God. It tells us that our nationality doesn't make one better than another. Our occupations or our social status does not matter. Being male or female does not make a difference. We are all one in Christ Jesus, therefore all are equal before God. If we could learn and practice this teaching, it would remove discrimination and we could all live better lives.

In the history of the church, there has been much debate over the role of women. The Scriptures in the letters of the Apostle Paul can appear very contradictory. In one letter, he is working with women as prophets and teachers, and in another writing, he tells them not even to ask a question. To understand the Scriptures, one has to look at the context of each writing. In one writing, he is speaking to women as prophets and teachers; in another, he is speaking about order during church meetings, within a specific culture. The wisdom of the Holy Spirit must be sought to help each person to understand Scripture as a whole.

Some Christian church denominations continue with the idea that only males can have certain leadership roles within the church. Could this be coming from faulty thinking rather than God? Should we not let our God, our Heavenly Father, define our calling? In the brokenness of human behavior, we often set barriers due to race, gender, societal status and our occupations. I would argue that this is not God's desire as we are all equal.

Chapter 8

Taking Charge

Individual Responsibility

Each of us has an important role and responsibility in the development of our individual futures. If we did not, my words would be useless and your attempts and mine would be counted as nothing. This is not the message of the Bible. The Bible was given by God not to take away our individual wills and freedoms to choose our paths, but to encourage and help us, and tell us how important we are to Him, a Holy God.

We all have our God given right to live out our lives and make our own choices. At the same time, we are not meant to drift with every thought that comes our way. We are taught in Scripture to take every thought captive. Getting carried away with our imaginations and emotions, can lead us down paths to disasters.

God will not force himself on our lives. It is our choice to submit our lives to a Holy God who loves us. Imagine what a difference it would make to trust in God, to rely on the Holy Spirit to reveal God's knowledge and wisdom for your life. One's life can become a journey of discovery and productivity in Christ.

Not only do we matter to God as individuals, but what we do as individuals matters to God. The Bible tells us that each person will give an account to God. This means we are personally responsible for what we do with our time on Earth. Each of us has to figure out how to live our lives best in the context of God's wisdom on their lives.

Outcomes

The Bible tells us we reap what we sow. This is an expression that is well understood by a farmer. If he plants carrot seeds, he will get carrots. Perhaps, he really wanted radishes. He will not receive radishes because he planted the wrong seed.

Accordingly, should we want to live without a heavy burden of debt, buying something we cannot afford will not produce the desired outcome. If we want to have a friend, we have to be caring and considerate and accept them flaws and all. Knowing that each decision produces consequences, seeking God's wisdom and knowledge is important.

Jesus Cares

The impact one has on others is important. Reading Matthew 25: 34 – 40, we find Jesus talking about the end times, using parables to show important truths to his disciples. Do we have a heart for those in need? It matters to our Lord. In the parable, Jesus was hungry and thirsty, he was a stranger, he needed clothing, he was sick, and he was in jail. One group helped him and one group did not. This parable tells us what Jesus expects from us. We are to care for others.

Being born again gives us salvation, and this is important. However, our salvation must bring us to love one another. What command did Jesus give us that covers all? Love God with all our heart, soul, and mind; and love our neighbor as we love ourselves. Following this command will please our Heavenly Father, and our reward will be a blessed life.

Moving Forward

We are at a very interesting and important period on Earth. Much history is behind us and we look forward not quite knowing what to expect. Knowing that God is good is an important fact to hold on to. Also keep in mind that Jesus came to give us peace. Not only any peace but peace that is beyond our understanding.

Learning from our past, both our successes and failures, we move forward. Each day is a new opportunity. Our attitude must take into consideration that we are children of God Almighty. Filling one's heart with joy and gladness, no matter what, is something to practice. It is very easy to fall into negative thinking and be critical of people and circumstances around us. We can rise above this. We are told to be thankful in everything because this pleases God. And do everything as unto the Lord. Following these tenets will help us to establish our peace. God wants us to seek his wisdom and do our best to make wise choices in an all circumstances.

The age in which we are living calls for added attention. Many in our world have limited knowledge of Jesus Christ. Believers have a truth and a hope that many just do not understand. We should not ignore those without understanding but pray for them and when opportunity comes, we are to share our faith. This must always be done with love in our hearts. Praying for others and keeping our hope in Christ Jesus, is pleasing to God.

Be a Leader

Being a leader is a privileged calling. Wanting to use one's leadership skills to help others can be difficult. One has to seek wisdom from God. Most importantly, being in leadership or just stepping out to work for God calls for perseverance. Often, leaders will have thoughts of discouragement and doubt and there will always be those who criticize. Expecting these challenges will enable one to continue on, knowing that God is always there for us. We must always be mindful that Satan opposes believers and specializes in pushing God's people to indulge in discouragement.

One's motivation has to be carefully checked. I have at times thought that I was doing something for God, only to realize that my motivation was wrong. I wanted to build myself up rather than give glory to God.

On one occasion, I learned a valuable lesson. Realizing that my motives were wrong, I started condemning myself and thinking I had to do better. The Spirit of God intervened and I quickly changed my thoughts. I began to thank God for bringing my prideful behavior out into the open so I could deal with it. I confessed my failings and asked him to take the pride away from me and he did. I now have more freedom to be who Christ wants me to be.

As we move through the complexities of life and work out who Christ wants us to be, there is always a right way and a wrong way of dealing with our personal issues. In the above example, I thank God's Spirit for giving me wisdom.

Power for Us

God's Word, the Holy Bible, must be our standard. To not find time for reading and thinking about it would be an opportunity missed. I suggest for one to live the best life possible and to have a good future requires trusting in Jesus. In order to trust Jesus, we must learn the many promises he wants to give us. Currently, through technology, we have the ability to stay in touch with others and the world at any time. Having so much information available to us is overwhelming and must be managed.

Holding fast to one's faith takes commitment. Your attention to your faith and to God will bring contentment and joy. Read your Bible daily. Send up your praises and sing songs. And talk to God from your heart. Let your requests be known and then forget about them. These practices will allow the God of the universe to be part of your earthy walk.

Joining a Bible study group, both for learning and social reasons is a good idea. Other believers can bring you wisdom and joy, and never forget no one is perfect, including yourself, so be patient! Yes, times are changing quickly. We need to take one day at a time and keep our focus on Jesus. We have been told that there will be a time of trouble and unfortunately, I believe we are now in the midst of it. Our role is to do what we feel led to do and leave the rest to God. Afterall, this earth and everything on it ultimately belongs to Him.

The real question we have to consider, especially as a Christian, is how should we proceed from here. In my view, it is especially important that we grow in knowing God and using our faith fully. We may not get another chance. Remember that Jesus told us that no one knows the day or the hour so we must be ready. Using these days strategically for yourself and others can make a difference for an eternity.

Chapter 9

Jews, Gentiles And The Sabbath Rest

One Plan for All

A key aspect of knowing God is to know his heart, his love for all humanity. God has a plan that brings Jews and Gentiles together in Christ.

Ephesians 2:12 – 16 (NIV)

> 12. Remember that at that time you were separate from Christ, excluded from citizenship in Israel and foreigners to the covenants of the promise, without hope and without God in the world.
> 13. But now in Christ Jesus you who once were far away have been brought near by the blood of Christ.
> 14. For he himself is our peace, who has made the two groups one and has destroyed the barrier, the dividing wall of hostility,

> 15. by setting aside in his flesh the law with its commands and regulations. His purpose was to create in himself one new humanity out of the two, thus making peace,
> 16. and in one body to reconcile both of them to God through the cross, by which he put to death their hostility.

What Happened

Paul, before he became a Christian, was a devout Jew who went by the name of Saul. His main goal as a Jew was to destroy the Christian faith. His life was changed when Jesus came to him on the road to Damascus. Jesus commissioned Paul to preach the gospel to the Gentiles. Jesus Christ came to save the lost and this included the Gentiles. But what happened to the Jews? Was it not Peter's mission to bring salvation to the Jews?

When we look at Israel today, we see a state divided between Judaism and secularism. They politely acknowledge Christians, but for the most part they reject Jesus with a passion. When you consider that the Gospel has spread all over the globe, it poses the question of why the Jews did not continue in the Christian faith? This is a complicated question. It is explained both in the Old and New testaments.

Sabbath Rest

Psalm 95 starts beautifully, by acknowledging God and praising him. The Psalm ends on a rather pessimistic note. It takes us back to the time in the wilderness when the Chosen People would not listen to God, even though they experienced all his power and miracles he had done for them. Psalm 95: 11, (NIV) *'So I declared an oath in my anger, 'they shall never enter my rest.'* What rest was God talking about?

Hebrews 4: 9, 10 (NIV)

> 9. There remains, then, a Sabbath-rest for the people of God;

10. for anyone who enters God's rest also rests from their works, just as God did from his.

In other words, believers are to no longer live their old lives; instead they are called to be co-workers with Jesus. After creation, God established the first Sabbath rest. He created for six days, and rested on the seventh. Why did he rest? He rested not because he was tired but because he had finished his work. This Sabbath rest of God was an example of a Sabbath rest that was to come. God asked the Chosen People to keep the Sabbath Holy by spending time with him. This Sabbath would be Saturday, the last day of the week. God gave ten commandments to Moses, one of which, is to remember the Sabbath and keep it holy. From the Jewish perspective, this continues today for those who practice their faith and follow the laws of Moses.

From the perspective of Jesus, the entire Church age is the new Sabbath rest. Not Sunday, or Saturday but every day. People who believe and follow Christ and submit to his Lordship, enter this new "Sabbath rest". We are finished with our former lives. Just as God had finished his work, we are to do likewise. Our new lives should become a Sabbath rest which is to follow Christ. However, one might consider setting aside Saturday, as this would be a continuum of God's will. Accordingly, how can the Jews have faith in Jesus, when in Psalm 95, it clearly states that "They shall never enter my rest"?

We as Christians know the only way to enter the true Sabbath Rest, is to do the will of Jesus Christ through our belief that he is the Son of God. The way for the Jewish people to enter this new Sabbath rest is the same, also through belief in Jesus Christ as Savior.

The Answer

The Book of Romans tells us some very interesting things about the situation of Israel. In Romans, Chapter 11, we find God's plan, the answer to this perplexing question.

Joyce Hum

Romans 11:12, 25 - 29 (NIV)

> 12. But if their transgression means riches for the world, and their loss means riches for the Gentiles, how much greater riches will their full inclusion bring!
> 25. I do not want you to be ignorant of this mystery, brothers and sisters, so that you may not be conceited: Israel has experienced a hardening in part until the full number of the Gentiles has come in,
> 26. and in this way all Israel will be saved. As it is written: "The deliverer will come from Zion; he will turn godlessness away from Jacob."
> 27. And this is my covenant with them when I take away their sins.
> 28. As far as the gospel is concerned, they are enemies for your sake; but as far as election is concerned, they are loved on account of the patriarchs,
> 29. for God's gifts and his call are irrevocable.

The above verses explain God's plan, that there would be a hardening in part among the Jews. This hardening allowed Gentiles the opportunity to become adopted into the faith of their God. We can now understand and should not be all that surprised by what appears to be rejection of Jesus Christ as their messiah. Verse 25, says *"until the full number of the Gentiles has come in."* Has the full number of the Gentiles occurred yet? God in his wisdom will know when this occurs. I believe that we will soon see many if not most Jewish people start believing the truth that Jesus Christ is their Messiah. Ephesians 2, 15,16 gives us the outcome of God's plan. *"His purpose was to create in himself one new humanity out of the two, (Jews and Gentiles) thus making peace, and in one body to reconcile both of them to God through the cross."* This is God's plan for all humanity. I am very excited knowing that God has a wonderful plan for his Chosen People. Soon and very soon we all will be one.

Chapter 10

The Time Is Near

Israel's Return

On May 14, 1948, the State of Israel was established. In 1947, the United Nations voted in favor of a plan to partition Palestine and allocate territory to create a homeland for the Jews. This decision allowed Israel to come back to the land that God gave them centuries ago. I believe the underlying reason for their decision was the terrible tragedy of six million Jews being murdered during World War Two. Israelites needed a safe place to call home.

The decision to give the Jews a nation, and not just any land, but the land that God gave them from the time of Abraham, had to happen. Otherwise, the end times prophecies could not be fulfilled. Jesus said when we see the tree budding (Israel's rebirth) that before this generation passes, he will return. What generation was he speaking about? I understand that a generation is seen as seventy years. Could this be referring to the people born after Israel became a nation state? It is now 72 years old. This sounds like a definite clue that the time is near.

Matthew 24: 32 – 35 (NIV)

> 32. Now learn this lesson from the fig tree: As soon as its twigs get tender and its leaves come out, you know that summer is near.
> 33. Even so, when you see all these things, you know that it is near, right at the door.
> 34. Truly I tell you, this generation will certainly not pass away until all these things have happened.
> 35. Heaven and earth will pass away, but my words will never pass away.

As in the Times of Noah and Lot

In the Book of Luke, Jesus was asked by the Pharisees when the kingdom of God would come. He answered that it would come as in the time of Noah and in the time of Lot. Noah lived in a sinful and violent world, probably only caring about themselves. Lot lived in the kingdom of Sodom.

Luke 17: 26 – 29 (NIV)

> 26. Just as it was in the days of Noah, so also will it be in the days of the Son of Man.
> 27. People were eating, drinking, marrying and being given in marriage up to the day Noah entered the ark. Then the flood came and destroyed them all.
> 28. was the same in the days of Lot. People were eating and drinking, buying and selling, planting and building.
> 29. But the day Lot left Sodom, fire and sulfur rained down from heaven and destroyed them all.

In the times of Noah and Lot people were living out their everyday lives but also doing things that were not pleasing to God. He brought judgement to them because he could only allow for so much disobedience. This implies that people will again be living in grave disobedience.

We are all sinners and God wants to forgive us. He saw our need for a Savior so he sent Jesus Christ who paid for all our sin. After I became a believer in Jesus, I began to see more clearly my many issues and it was discouraging. However, I also saw changes. I began to see people differently. I realized their value and how important each person is to God. Instead of judging, I now pray for myself and for others. We all need the power of a Holy God living within to help us grow in goodness.

Like Jeremiah who was a prophet called by God to tell the Israelites to stop worshipping idols, I too, ask for God's grace for me and all of humanity to seek God with repentance. There are many who have taken this opportunity to heart, and I believe many more will follow.

The Parable of the Ten Virgins

In Matthew 24, Jesus has a discussion with his disciples concerning when he will return. This is followed in Matthew 25, with Jesus telling parables about the Kingdom of Heaven. One story that came to my attention is the story about the ten brides, referred to as virgins. Five were foolish and five were wise. The important thing to notice is that all were aware that the groom would be coming. The five who were not wise did not have enough oil to keep their lamps burning. They had to leave to buy more oil. When they returned, it was too late. The groom had come and they missed their opportunity. Fifty percent did not get to go with the groom. I believe Jesus gave us this story as a caution.

Matthew 25: 1 – 13 (NIV)

> 1. At that time the kingdom of heaven will be like ten virgins who took their lamps and went out to meet the bridegroom.
> 2. Five of them were foolish and five were wise.
> 3. The foolish ones took their lamps but did not take any oil with them.
> 4. The wise ones, however, took oil in jars along with their lamps.

5. The bridegroom was a long time in coming, and they all became drowsy and fell asleep.
6. At midnight the cry rang out: 'Here's the bridegroom! Come out to meet him!'
7. Then all the virgins woke up and trimmed their lamps.
8. The foolish ones said to the wise, 'Give us some of your oil; our lamps are going out.'
9. 'No,' they replied, 'there may not be enough for both us and you. Instead, go to those who sell oil and buy some for yourselves.'
10. But while they were on their way to buy the oil, the bridegroom arrived. The virgins who were ready went in with him to the wedding banquet. And the door was shut.
11. Later the others also came. 'Lord, Lord,' they said, 'open the door for us!'
12. But he replied, 'Truly I tell you, I don't know you.'
13. Therefore, keep watch, because you do not know the day or the hour.

There is a wide difference between knowing about Jesus at an intellectual level and knowing him at a spiritual level. We need a personal relationship with Jesus. We need to be born again, this time by the Holy Spirit of God. I believe our spiritual relationship is synonymous with the oil. Do we have a spiritual relationship with Jesus? This comes when we accept him as Lord and Savior of our lives.

Going back to the ten virgins, only five went with Jesus. Does this mean the virgins left behind will miss out on eternal salvation? They might and they might not. The parable does not say they are lost forever. Might they get another chance? I believe they will, but it would be in a difficult period, the rule of earth by the beast.

This Day Will Come

Who will be included? When we study the parable of the ten virgins, we see that fifty percent were not ready. Christians have to be ready. We want our lamps burning brightly when the call comes. The Christians who are ready, will not have to wait outside the door of the wedding banquet.

Looking again at the parable of the Ten Virgins, what lesson do we need to learn. I believe the parable tells Christians, just knowing about Jesus is not enough. We need to accept Jesus as our personal Lord and Savior. In other words, we must have submitted lives. We have to be born again as Jesus told Nicodemus in John 3. Those who are born again by the Spirit, will be granted admittance to the wedding banquet.

I believe the parable of the virgins is about meeting Jesus in the air. Christians refer to this as the rapture. This word is not used in the Bible, but it is clearly described in two places in the Bible. These are our encouragement.

1 Thessalonians 4: 13-18 (NIV)

> 13. Brothers and sisters, we do not want you to be uninformed about those who sleep in death, so that you do not grieve like the rest of mankind, who have no hope.
> 14. For we believe that Jesus died and rose again, and so we believe that God will bring with Jesus those who have fallen asleep in him.
> 15. According to the Lord's word, we tell you that we who are still alive, who are left until the coming of the Lord, will certainly not precede those who have fallen asleep.
> 16. For the Lord himself will come down from heaven, with a loud command, with the voice of the archangel and with the trumpet call of God, and the dead in Christ will rise first.

> 17. After that, we who are still alive and are left will be caught up together with them in the clouds to meet the Lord in the air. And so we will be with the Lord forever.
> 18. Therefore encourage one another with these words.

This Scripture tells us that the Christians who have already died will have their bodies again. Before this, they were with Jesus but with a spiritual body. They will have a resurrected body so they can come to Earth and reign with Jesus. We who are alive, will be caught up together with them in the clouds and meet our Lord in the air. This event is also referred to in the Book of Revelation 3:10, in the message to the Church of Philadelphia, believers are told they will be taken away to protect them from the hour of trial. We must be ready to be raptured. Having a born-again relationship with Jesus, we can be ready to meet Jesus in the air. We do not have to experience the terrible time on earth under the rule of the Beast, the hour of trial.

Chapter 11

Deception

Its Meaning

Yes, the time is near for the return of Jesus. In Matthew 24, Jesus speaks about his return. He starts by warning his followers to not be deceived. What did he mean, and why is this warning so important? It is important because deception can lead us away from the truth of God's Word and could ultimately lead to losing our salvation.

Have you ever been deceived? I know I have. All I can say is thank you Lord Jesus for not granting my every prayer request. Instead, you sent me your wisdom. I fall into deception when I really want something to be. I wish I had a better report but the truth of it is, I don't.

I have tried to be part of specific groups where, after serious thought, I moved away from. I have also wanted to do great things for God, only to later come to the conclusion that it was only me trying to glorify myself. Pride can be a ruthless taskmaster.

So, what is deception? Deception is a lie that we believe as truth. That's what makes deception so dangerous. Based on circumstances and influences around us, we like what we hear and this becomes our truth. Once a deception becomes our truth it can be very difficult to move away from. We like our truths even if they are not truths. This is because we are comfortable with familiarity. We would rather live with a lie than suffer the emotional torments of accepting truths. These lies come easily, often as part of our culture and tradition. However, I boldly say that both culture and tradition are very real threats. Threats that can prevent us from having a personal relationship with Jesus Christ as our Lord and Savior.

Deception is a tool of Satan, neither individuals nor churches are excluded. It is so easy to fall into traditions and practices mainly because they are passed down as a birth right. People also join in because they want to be part of something bigger than themselves. The outcome of this is serious. They lose touch with the power of God by not paying attention or knowing the truth found in the Word of God.

False teaching is any belief or practice that is not based on the Word of God, or in extreme cases, is even contrary to the Word of God. False teaching originates from different sources. It can be adopted from others without scrutiny, or originate from popular and charismatic leaders. False teaching is man-made and dangerous because it replaces Biblical truths. We should pay attention to the Words of Jesus in Revelation 22:7 *"Look, I am coming soon! Blessed is the one who keeps the words of the prophecy written in this scroll."*

When we stand before Jesus, telling him we belonged to a particular denomination will not impress him. The bottom line for our acceptance into eternity and having our names recorded in the Lamb's Book of Life, is our belief in Jesus Christ. In other words, as Jesus told Nicodemus, in John 3, we have to be born again by the Spirit of God and this happens through our belief in Jesus Christ.

Our Responsibility

In Philippians 2, we are told that each person must work out their salvation with fear and trembling. The expression "fear and trembling" refers to us having a proper relationship with God our creator. The word "fear" refers to us approaching God with all due respect, while the word "trembling" refers to us having personal humility when acknowledging our failures and need of a Savior.

Philippians 2: 12-13 (NIV)

> 12. Therefore, my dear friends, as you have always obeyed - not only in my presence, but now much more in my absence - continue to work out your salvation with fear and trembling,
> 13. for it is God who works in you to will and to act in order to fulfill his good purpose.

Your faith and salvation belong to you as an individual. We must be ready to stand before God as an individual, and give an account of what we did with our lives. Living life is both an opportunity and a responsibility to be a co-worker with God, for it is God who works in you to will and to act in order to fulfill his good purpose.

Being part of a Bible believing church is beneficial. Learning about God and his Word, and belonging to a church family, are comforting. However, never allow teaching and practices to trump the written Word of God.

I have had experiences that taught me valuable lessons. What about a church that becomes so prideful that they begin to think they are better than others? This becomes a church built on pride of men rather than the love of God. What about a church that says it is infallible and we are to call the leader Holy Father? Another grave disrespect for a Holy God.

There are many false teachings out there. Once, I encountered a teaching that taught something very different than the Bible. The teaching held that all people on earth will become Christians before the second coming of Jesus Christ. In order to believe this, one would have to deny the words of Jesus in the Gospels and the Book of Revelation, and not accept the prophecies of Daniel nor many other prophecies found in the Old Testament. Revelation 20: 7-10, tells us that even after the thousand-year reign of Jesus Christ, many will turn away. Satan will be allowed once more to roam the earth and again many will join him. This is the Word of God.

In addition, many "prophets" are telling us that God is about to bring complete salvation to North America. Are these prophets from God? Jesus tells us in Matthew 24:10 that many will turn away from the faith. Did Jesus get it wrong? Are born again believers increasing in North America? Are not many churches being torn down or used for different purposes? I would like to jump on this band wagon of false teaching because it all sounds good. However, the Word of the living God must be my standard. I too, will be held accountable to God.

Deception is very possible. Matthew 24:4, *"Watch out that no one deceives you."* must be taken seriously. The biggest danger of being deceived is our lack of knowledge from the Bible. Otherwise we open ourselves to deception. Our enemy wants us to make poor decisions, to do and say things that will lead us away from truth. So beware, there is a powerful force that has the mandate to keep us in deception. The root of deception comes from Satan who roams the earth and knows our weaknesses. The power of deception can creep in easily.

We are the Bride of Christ. We must hold fast to the Word of God. There is no other way to be part of the truth and have our names written in the Lamb's Book of Life.

Chapter 12

Pay Attention To Biblical Prophecies

Knowledge of Future Truths

The study of the end times is called eschatology. A somewhat unusual word. My first impression when I heard this word was confusion. What does this word mean? It is my understanding it means the science of last things. The question that came to mind is this word appropriate? Are we studying last things?

I have a different view of the Biblical account of the end times. From my perspective, they are about new beginnings and a new hope. However, before we come to the exciting and miraculous future God has for us, there is a path to tread.

Importance of Prophecies

2 Peter 1: 19 - 21 (NIV)

> 19. We also have the prophetic message as something completely reliable, and you will do well to pay attention to it, as to a light shining in a dark place, until the day dawns and the morning star rises in your hearts.
> 20. Above all, you must understand that no prophecy of Scripture came about by the prophet's own interpretation of things.
> 21. For prophecy never had its origin in the human will, but prophets, though human, spoke from God as they were carried along by the Holy Spirit.

Biblical prophecies are words spoken by men but given by God. Many prophecies have been fulfilled. Others are yet to come. I firmly believe that all Biblical prophecies will be fulfilled. They are future truths written to give knowledge and understanding to the reader. I believe that everyone should read them and take them to heart. Knowledge about what to expect in the future is important. God wants us to have hope. We get hope by knowing what is ahead and trusting God to help us in our struggles.

Jesus himself was not popular with the ruling class and suffered severe persecution. All of his apostles, including Paul suffered cruel deaths. The only exception was John, and he died alone on the Isle of Patmos. Even today, followers of Christ around the world are ostracized, beaten, put in jail and even killed.

In Canada and the United States, we are fortunate to live in countries where laws are upheld, and people have freedom of religion. The big question is whether freedom of religion will continue to be upheld. Speaking the truth, and trying to live a righteous life, often gets one in trouble. No matter the circumstances, Christians are to trust in a holy and loving God, knowing eternal life awaits us.

End Time Prophecies

In the Old Testament, end time prophecies are found in Daniel, and the books of the prophets, especially Ezekiel. In the New Testament, end time prophecies are found in Matthew 24 and Luke 17. In these chapters, Jesus answers questions posed by his disciples and the Pharisees. The last book of the New Testament is the Revelation of Jesus Christ.

All prophecies work together to give us a better understanding. Ezekiel, Daniel, Revelation, and the words of Jesus, all help us to understand what will occur in the future. We can have a keen expectation of the days ahead. Some of the imagery is difficult to comprehend; however, the intent of messages is clear. The Prophecies of Daniel are introduced first, as they provide foundational explanations for those of Revelation.

End time prophecies cover the last seven years of man's reign on Earth and beyond. As we look into these last seven years of man's reign, the events are disturbing and I find myself asking the question if they are preventable. I don't think they are. However, God knows everything and this includes the future. As such, he shares the future with us through the prophets. He wants us to be prepared and that is a good thing. This last seven-year period is divided into two equal parts, with the latter being a terrible time upon Earth. This period is relatively short. After which we have the second coming of our Savior, Jesus Christ. Amen.

Chapter 13

Prophecies Of Daniel

Daniel in Babylonia

The prophecies of Daniel contain information on the Israelites that cover a span from Babylon to and including the end times. These prophecies, together with the Book of Revelation, show us the future and its challenges. However, they also show that Almighty God knows all.

The Book of Daniel tells the story of Hebrew young men, including Daniel, who were captured by the Babylonians and taken to Babylonia around 609 BC. Judah came under siege by the Babylonians three times. Jerusalem and the temple were destroyed ending the nation of Judah in 587 BC. Daniel was taken captive during the first siege and served under both the Babylonians and the Persians. Daniel, while in captivity did not give up his faith. He remained steadfast and sought God on behalf of his country through determined prayers. God answered Daniel's prayers and he is given hope for the future of his people.

This chapter examines four of Daniel's prophecies.

1. King Nebuchadnezzar's Dream
2. Daniel's Dream of Four Beasts
3. Daniel's Seventy "Sevens"
4. The King of the North and the King of the South

Each of the prophecies is a major step in understanding the history of man and God's plan for the end times. Annex A, Four Prophecies of Daniel, found at the end of this book can be viewed to further help with understanding their end time significance.

1. King Nebuchadnezzar's Dream

King Nebuchadnezzar of Babylonia had a dream which concerned him, so he asked his wise men to tell him the dream as well as give him the interpretation. None could help him. Daniel went to the King and asked for time, he explained that there is God of Heaven who will help him. After prayer, God told Daniel the dream as well as its interpretation. (See Daniel 2: 26 – 45) Daniel tells the King what he dreamt; it was a dream of an enormous statue. The statue had a head of gold, its chest and arms of silver, its belly and thighs of bronze. It had legs of iron, its feet and toes were partly of iron, and partly of baked clay. While the king watched, a large rock was cut out but not by human hands. The rock struck the statue on its feet and all of it was broken into pieces. The rock that struck the statue became a large mountain and filled the whole earth.

Daniel continued with the interpretation:

Daniel 2: 38 – 43 (NIV)

> 38. "......You are that head of gold.
> 39. After you, another kingdom will arise (silver) inferior to yours. Next, a third kingdom, one of bronze, will rule over the whole earth.
> 40. Finally, there will be a fourth kingdom, strong as iron – for iron breaks and smashes everything – and as

> iron breaks things to pieces, so it will crush and break all the others.
>
> 41. Just as you saw that the feet and toes were partly of baked clay and partly of iron, so this will be a divided kingdom; yet it will have some of the strength of iron in it, even as you saw iron mixed with clay.
>
> 42. As the toes were partly iron and partly clay, so this kingdom will be partly strong and partly brittle.
>
> 43. And just as you saw the iron mixed with baked clay, so the people will be a mixture and will not remain united, any more than iron mixes with clay.

Historical Perspective

The statue represented all the major empires of the world which were to come. The Babylon Empire was the golden head. The empire represented by the silver chest and arms followed, these were the Medes and Persian Empire. Next came the bronze belly and thighs, which were the Greek Empire. The iron legs were the Roman Empire. This empire of iron took over the entire area by crushing the others. The feet and toes are made of clay mixed with iron, as they are influenced by Rome. The feet and toes would be the last remaining powers of man's rule.

Prophetic Perspective

Daniel 2: 44, 45 (NIV)

> 44. In the time of those kings, the God of heaven will set up a kingdom that will never be destroyed, nor will it be left to another people. It will crush all those kingdoms and bring them to an end, but it will itself endure forever.
>
> 45. This is the meaning of the vision of the rock cut out of a mountain, but not by human hands—a rock that broke the iron, the bronze, the clay, the silver and the gold to pieces.

> The great God has shown the king what will take place in the future. The dream is true and its interpretation is trustworthy.

The large statue covers all the years of man's reign from the Babylonians to the present time. The end comes in the above Scriptures. *"In the time of those kings,"* these are the two feet and the ten toes. At this period of time God will intervene. Jesus Christ will return to earth as a mighty warrior. At Armageddon, he will be victorious. *"The God of heaven will set up a kingdom that will never be destroyed."* Jesus Christ will crush all the kingdoms (the ten toes) and bring them to an end. He is the large rock and he will rule the entire earth. The Book of Revelation tells us that His earthy kingdom will lead to the New Jerusalem, which never ends.

Some Biblical commentators have come to the conclusion that the feet and the ten toes tells us the Roman Empire will rise again, and have rule over ten nation states. I differ in my opinion. As part of the two feet and ten toes, countries emerged in Europe in the nineteenth century and established empires around the world. Over the past two millennia, the church in Rome has spread and established itself in countries around the world. The iron is mixed with the clay. I believe this is the continued influence of Rome. Could the explanation for the two feet and ten toes be God seeing our earth as we see it today? The two feet (two major land masses) and ten toes could represent all places on earth where people live, and signify that the prophecy will extend to all corners of the world.

I especially take into consideration the final words of this prophecy in Daniel 2: 45: *"The great God has shown the King what will take place in the future. The dream is true and the interpretation is trustworthy."*

2. Daniel's Dream of Four Beasts

Daniel 7: 1 (NIV)

> 1. In the first year of Belshazzar king of Babylon, Daniel had a dream, and visions passed through his mind as he

was lying in bed. He wrote down the substance of his dream.

In Chapter 7, verses 1 to 14, Daniel describes his dream. In his dream, he sees four beasts come out of the sea. One resembled a lion, another a bear, and another a leopard. The fourth beast was not described as an animal. It was different than the others. It had iron teeth and crushed and devoured its victims. This beast had ten horns. Among the ten horns, a little horn appears.

Daniel 7: 8 (NIV)

8. While I was thinking about the horns, there before me was another horn, a little one, which came up among them; and three of the first horns were uprooted before it. This horn had eyes like the eyes of a human being and a mouth that spoke boastfully.

Daniel is given a glorious vision of Jesus. Daniel 7: 13 "In my vision at night I looked, and there before me was one like a son of man, coming with the clouds of heaven."

This is followed by a man who interprets his dream. Four kings will rise up from the earth. The fourth kingdom will be different from the others and it will devour the whole earth. Ten horns will arise, and then a little horn which will be different from the others.

In Chapter 7, verses 21 to 25, we are told there will be a war against the holy people of God (Jews) and they will be defeated until the Ancient of Days (Jesus) comes. The holy people will be delivered into the hands of the little horn for a time, times and half a time. (three and one-half years). But Jesus will destroy the little horn and the people of the Most-High will receive the kingdom and keep it forever.

Historical Perspective

Here we are presented with four beasts, who are four kings. To understand this dream, one again has to look at history. Going back to the statue in Nebuchadnezzar's dream, the four beasts have the same meaning as the four parts of the statue. The four beasts represent Babylon, Medes and Persians, Greece and Rome. Rome is the fourth and it is not given a name of an animal. It is more dangerous than the others, it is made of iron and crushes others.

Many commentators believe that the ten horns represent European countries under the control of Rome at a point of time in history. The little horn comes up among the ten horns, it is part of Rome but something small.

The Roman Empire is no longer, however, countries in Europe have fought each other, and since World War Two, sought peace and prosperity by forming the European Union.

In 313 CE, the Roman Emperor Constantine legalized Christianity and in 330 CE moved the capital to Constantinople. This left the Roman church as the central authority in Rome. The church spread and became a major religion around the world. The church in Rome is a sovereign entity recognized by international treaty in 1929 and is accorded diplomatic status similar to a country.

Prophetic Perspective

Daniel 7:25 - 27 (NIV)

> 25. He will speak against the Most High and oppress his holy people and try to change the set times and the laws. The holy people will be delivered into his hands for a time, times and half a time.
> 26. But the court will sit, and his power will be taken away and completely destroyed forever.

> 27. Then the sovereignty, power and greatness of all the kingdoms under heaven will be handed over to the holy people of the Most High. His kingdom will be an everlasting kingdom, and all rulers will worship and obey him.

To put this into context, one has to go back to the large statue of Nebuchadnezzar's dream. The two feet and ten toes that are made partly of iron and partly of clay. These are the existing nations on the earth just before the end times. The little horn comes from the fourth kingdom, which is Rome. The little horn has enormous power and influence and gets itself in a position of authority and influence among all existing nations.

It speaks boastfully against God and oppresses the holy people. In verse 25, we see that it oppresses the holy people, meaning the chosen people of Israel, for the three and one-half-year period (time, times and half a time). This is the same length of time given in other end time prophecies, indicating the reign of the beast. Verse 26, tells us that after the three and one-half year period the court will sit. And the power of the little horn will be taken away from it. The power will be handed over to the Holy people.

To conclude this explanation, I go back to Daniel 7: 11. Here Daniel sees God on his throne, and a court room. As Daniel watched, this little horn, now referred to as a beast, is slain and thrown into a blazing fire. Then one like the son of man (Jesus Christ), enters the throne room and is given an everlasting dominion. This is explained further in Revelation 19:19. Jesus Christ will return to earth as a mighty warrior. The beast and the false prophet are thrown into a lake of fire, and Jesus Christ is given an everlasting dominion. Thereby giving us the fulfillment of Daniel's prophecy.

3) Daniel's Seventy "Sevens"

Daniel 9: 18 – 25 (NIV)

God often uses the number seven to indicate when something is complete. For example, God uses the number seven with creation, which includes his last day where he rested. Accordingly, whenever we see the number seven; we can try and find out what has been completed, or how long it will take to complete.

Daniel says a prayer of confession to God and asks him for mercy for his people. At the end of verse 9:18, Daniel prays "......*We do not make requests of you because we are righteous, but because of your great mercy."* In response to Daniel's prayer, the angel Gabriel came to him, in verses 9: 24 - 26

> 24. Seventy 'sevens' are decreed for your people and your holy city to finish transgression, to put an end to sin, to atone for wickedness to bring in everlasting righteousness, to seal up vision and prophecy and to anoint the Most Holy Place.

Here the angel is speaking in years. The word 'sevens' refers to a period on seven years. Therefore, seventy 'sevens'. This calculates out to four hundred and ninety years. This is an amazing prophecy. It says that all that needs to be completed, will be completed during the four hundred and ninety years and the end result will be everlasting righteousness. The angel, however, goes on to give more detail:

> 25. Know and understand this: From the time the word goes out to restore and rebuild Jerusalem until the Anointed One, the ruler, comes, there will be seven 'sevens' and sixty-two 'sevens'. It will be rebuilt with streets and a trench, but in times of trouble.
> 26. After the sixty-two 'sevens' the Anointed One will be put to death and will have nothing...

The message from the angel gives us the time frame for the fulfillment of this prophecy. From the time when Nehemiah returned to Jerusalem in 445 B.C. to rebuild the walls, to the entry of the Anointed One (Jesus) there will be seven, sevens (7X7 = 49) years and sixty-two sevens (62X7 = 434) years. which gives us a total of four hundred and eighty-three years

(49+ 434 = 483). I am not sure why this is divided in two parts. However, the forty-nine years was likely the period of rebuilding.

Historical Perspective

The Chosen People were in captivity in Babylonia for seventy years. The exact timing God gave Jeremiah in a prophecy. After the seventy years, God spoke to Cyrus, the king of Persia, and told him to allow the Chosen People to return to Jerusalem. Ezra returned and rebuilt the city and Nehemiah returned and rebuilt the wall. Jesus Christ, the anointed one, was born in Bethlehem, and had an amazing ministry.

Prophetic Perspective

After the seventy years in Babylonia, the Chosen People did return and rebuilt the temple and the wall in Jerusalem as prophesied. From the time Nehemiah left Babylon, to the coming of the Anointed One (Jesus Christ) would be four hundred and eighty-three years. Depending on the start date, this was fulfilled (Matthew 21:11) when Jesus rode into Jerusalem on the foal of a donkey. Zechariah 9:9 also prophesied the coming of a king: *"righteous and victorious, lowly and riding on a donkey, on a colt, the foal of a donkey."* Jesus was crucified five days later, completing what the Angel Gabriel told Daniel. A useful resource on this can be found in Enduringword.com. 7. It provides an analysis of Biblical commentators and their calculations on the 483 years leading up to the entry of Jesus into Jerusalem.

The first period of the 483 years concluded with Jesus riding into Jerusalem, his trial, his death by crucifixion and his resurrection. However, there remains the last 'one sevens'. Before his ascension back to his Father, Jesus gave his followers the great commission. They are to go out into the world and preach the good news of salvation. This period of preaching the great commission is referred to as the church age. Accordingly, there are two thousand plus years in between the first four hundred and eighty-three years and the last 'one seven' years.

Daniel's prayers and answers to his prayers always pertain to the Chosen People and their homeland. The nation of Israel will again be prominent in the seven years of the end times. This last seven years takes place just before the second coming of Jesus Christ. The explanation is given in the Scripture below. There is yet to be, the seven years of end time tribulations.

Daniel 9: 27 (NIV)

> 27. He will confirm a **covenant with many for one 'seven.' In the middle of the 'seven'** he will put an end to sacrifice and offering. And at the temple he will set up an abomination that causes desolation, until the end that is decreed is poured out on him."

4. The Kings of the South and the North

Daniel 10 & 11 (NIV)

This prophecy begins in Chapter 10 and continues in Chapter 11. Daniel receives a revelation in a vision and its interpretation. This prophecy is about major powers, that engage in conflicts to gain and maintain control. These powers are those residing in the South and the powers residing in the North. In Daniel 10: 21, while he was standing by the River Tigris, a man clothed in linen spoke to him; *"but first I will tell you what is written in the Book of Truth."*

In Daniel's first prophecy of Nebuchadnezzar's dream of a large statue, different empires emerge leading to the two feet and the ten toes. These are the empires Daniel's would be describing in this prophecy on the Kings of the South and the Kings of the North. During most of this period in history Israel was not a nation state.

In Daniel 11: 21, the wording changes and dialogue on the end times commences. During the end times, this prophecy on the conflict between the two kings takes into consideration the message given to Daniel by the Angel Gabriel, on the Seventy 'sevens', where the one 'sevens' (seven years) remain (Daniel 9:27). This is the last seven years of man's reign of earth and referred to as the end times. It is a time where Israel again plays a pivotal role in God's plan for the earth.

Daniel 11: 21 – 24 (NIV)

> 21: He will be succeeded by a contemptible person who has not been given the honor of royalty. He will invade the kingdom when its people feel secure, and he will seize it through intrigue.
> 22: Then an overwhelming army will he swept away before him; both it and a prince of the covenant will be destroyed.
> 23: After coming to an agreement with him, he will act deceitfully, and with only a few people he will rise to power.
> 24: When the richest provinces feel secure, he will invade them and will achieve what nether his fathers nor his forefathers did. He will distribute plunder, loot and wealth among his followers. He will plot the overthrow of fortresses – but only for a time.

This King of the North, is not a king of royalty, instead he is a person of authority and commands attention. He is well respected and but very deceitful, as he seizes the kingdom through intrigue. In verse 22, the overwhelming army, meaning the army of Israel, is swept away and an important person of faith will be removed. In verse 23, the King of the North will start small with only a few people but will rise to power. Through his ability to lead, many will follow him. "When the richest provinces feel secure, he will invade them."

Daniel 11: 31 – 33 (NIV)

> 31. His armed forces will rise up to desecrate the temple fortress and will abolish the daily sacrifice. Then they will set up the abomination that causes desolation.

> 32. With flattery he will corrupt those who have violated the covenant, but the people who know their God will firmly resist him.
> 33. Those who are wise will instruct many, though for a time they will fall by the sword or be burned or captured or plundered.

Verse 11: 31 shows the power and determination of the king of the North to take away practices that are important to the Holy people. He will put an end to the daily sacrifice and set up an abomination that causes desolations. In verse 32, his power to flatter people becomes apparent as he gets people to follow him. Verse 33 is an encouragement to those who continue to instruct people in the truth of God's Word, these brave people are referred to as wise. We are also told of the brutality of this king when he is disobeyed.

Daniel 12: 7 (NIV)

> 7. The man clothed in linen, who was above the waters of the river, lifted his right hand and his left hand toward heaven, and I heard him swear by him who lives forever, saying, "It will be for a time, times and half a time. When the power of the holy people has been finally broken, all these things will be completed."

In Daniel 12, the dialogue between Daniel and the angel continues. In verse 5, Daniel sees two others. In verse 12: 6, one of the men asked the man dressed in linen how long it would be before all these things would be fulfilled. His answer repeats and verifies what was said in Daniel 9:27, in the middle of the one seven, meaning seven years divided by two; an evil ruler would set up his reign for three and one-half years.

Historical Perspective

History tell us that the fourth kingdom, the Roman Empire is finished. However, we have the past prophecies of Daniel to draw upon. From

Nebuchadnezzar's dream we have all the world's empires including Rome, which is made of iron. The influence of Rome, the iron mixes with feet and toes of clay. The feet and toes represent the nations of the end times. In the prophecy of Daniel and the four beasts, we are told the fourth beast, Rome, is more terrifying than the others. Rome has control over ten countries and among the countries a little horn (a small country) comes up.

Daniel 7: 25, 26 (NIV)

> 25. He (the little horn) will speak against the Most High and oppress his holy people and try to change the set times and the laws. The holy people will be delivered into his hands for a time, times, and half a time.
> 26. But the court will sit, and his power will be taken away and completely destroyed forever.

The little horn becomes very powerful and deceitful. I believe the little horn at this time is the king of the North. This is developed further in the following chapter on the Prophecies of Revelation.

Prophetic Perspective

In Daniel's interpretation of king Nebuchadnezzar's dream, we have the iron mixed with the clay of the ten toes, meaning the entire world. The Roman Empire is no longer, however, countries in Europe have formed the European Union to coordinate their economies and wield influence on the world stage. The church in Rome is established around the world and speaks to world issues.

In Daniel 7, we have Daniel's Dream of four beasts. In the interpretation, these become four kings who come out of the earth. The fourth, which is the Roman Empire, comes with ten and the little horn. The little horn had the eyes of a human and a mouth that spoke boastfully and was more imposing than the others. In Daniel 7: 21, this horn wages war against the holy people and defeats them. Daniel 7: 25 ……. *"The holy people will be delivered into his hands for a time, times and one half a time. 7:26, But the court will sit and his power will be taken away and completely destroyed forever."*

In Daniel 12, the man dressed in linen (whom I believe to be Jesus Christ) gave specific information to Daniel on the timing. This timing is the same as Daniel 7: 25. The king of the North will rule from the Temple in Jerusalem for three and one-half years (for a time, times and one half a time). This is the last three and one-half years of the "one sevens", referred to in Daniel 9. These, I believe are the last seven years of man's reign on earth, that ends with the reign of the evil King of the North, the little horn, the Beast of Revelation, who are one and the same.

Chapter 14

The Revelation Of Jesus Christ

The Final Truth

Revelation, is the last book of the New Testament. It was written by the Apostle John, around 95 AD. Jesus, while on earth, chose twelve men to walk with him. Jesus was crucified, buried in a rich man's tomb, and he returned to life on the third day after his death. After forty days, he ascended into the clouds to sit at the right hand of his Father.

His apostles continued telling people about Jesus but they paid a high price. Eleven were murdered, and John was placed on a barren Island called Patmos and left to die. While on the Island, Jesus sent an angel to John. The angel tells and shows John many things. He tells him to write all on a scroll. Hence, we have the Revelation of Jesus Christ.

Important Knowledge

Before writing on Revelation, I read different Bible commentaries to seek advice. I found some commentaries that questioned if the book, Revelation, should have even been included in the Bible. I believe this book is very important to God. This is made clear by reading the Prologue:

Revelation 1: 1-3 (NIV)

> 1. The revelation from Jesus Christ, which God gave him to show his servants what must soon take place. He made it known by sending his angel to his servant John,
> 2. who testifies to everything he saw – that is, the word of God and the testimony of Jesus Christ.
> 3. Blessed is the one who reads aloud the words of this prophecy, and blessed are those who hear it and take to heart what is written in it, because the time is near.

I believe it is important to read Revelation. Struggle as we may, making it part of one's Christian education will give us very important knowledge we need to know. As events unfold, being prepared and knowing what will come, will help us to fully realize the awesome outcome of serving a Holy God, and our Lord Jesus Christ. Qualifying for a promised future that God wants no one to miss, is our goal. Accordingly, I encourage all to continue learning and stay steadfast in the power of God. Be informed and ready for the days ahead. I certainly recommend that people read the Book of Revelation in its entirety.

The following discourses set out my understanding and thoughts on specific events found in the Book of Revelation. These were carefully chosen to show God's path forward for the future. I felt compelled to write these discourses, believing the power of God is with me.

Ten Discourses on the Book of Revelation

The events or happenings are as follows:

1. Woes - Before the Reign of the Beasts, (the first three and one-half years)

2. Meeting Jesus in the Air, (a point in time)
3. The Two Beasts, and their Reign, (the last three and one-half years)
4. The Fall of Babylon, (a point in time)
5. The Second Coming of Jesus Christ, (a point in time)
6. The Reign of Jesus Christ on Earth, (one thousand years)
7. Satan's Return and the Last Falling Away, (for a short time)
8. The Judgement of the Dead, (a point in time)
9. The End of Time as We Know It, (a point in time)
10. A New Place Appears – New Jerusalem, (for eternity)

Annex B provides a summary of the Book of Revelation.

1. Woes – Before the Reign of the Beasts, (the first three and one-half years)

Revelation includes messages for seven churches in chapters 2 and 3. These were actual churches in Asia. All churches today should read the messages and learn from them. In chapters 6 to 11, a scroll with seven seals is opened by the Lamb of God. The seventh seal reveals seven trumpets that are to be sounded by angels.

In Revelation 6:1-17, the seals are opened one at a time. From the first four seals, comes Four horses, each a different color and having different attributes. These are powers roaming the earth. In Revelation 6:12-14, a great earthquake is described. The earthquake appears to be the same earthquake found in Revelation 16:18-20.

In chapter 8, the seventh seal is opened, standing before God are seven angels, each with a trumpet. In turn each angel sounds a trumpet. After each of the first four trumpets sounds, a woe occurs on the earth. Each woe affects one third of the world with hail, fire, a mountain falls into the sea, and one third of the sun and moon become dark. In chapter 9, the fifth trumpet sounds and a star fall onto the earth. It has the key to the shaft of the abyss. Things like scorpions and locusts are released from the abyss, these torture people for five months. When the sixth trumpet sounds four angels are released to kill a third of mankind. Many troops come on the scene and the following description speaks of horses and riders, and weapons of war. In chapter 11, the seventh trumpet sounds, a loud voice in heaven announces that the World's kingdom has now become the Kingdom of our God.

Observations

Reading about the woes leaves me with unanswered questions, the main question being why? Have any already occurred? Can they be taken literally or are they symbolic of woes in general. I cannot answer these questions. However, we are currently living in tumultuous times. Violence, diseases, climate issues, locusts, fires and economic uncertainty are very real. Could the God of heaven be trying to get our attention? Could it be that our tumultuous times are part of these prophesied woes? The Scriptures below tell us God wants none to perish.

2 Peter 3: 8 – 9 (NIV)

> 8. But do not forget this one thing, dear friends: With the Lord a day is like a thousand years, and a thousand years are like a day.
> 9. The Lord is not slow in keeping his promise, as some understand slowness. Instead he is patient with you, not wanting anyone to perish, but everyone to come to repentance.

Sometimes when all is going well, we may not realize our need for God or a Savior. Remember that God is a God of wisdom.

The big question is Are We There Yet? Can we equate our current woes with the end time prophecies? I believe, especially looking back at our recent past, we may have already entered this period. Should I be correct in my belief, the next major event we have to be ready for is discussed below.

2. Meeting Jesus in the Air, (a point in time)

Messages were given to each of seven churches in Asia. Only one, the Church of Philadelphia, was told that they would be kept away from the hour of trial. The hour of trial is coming, meaning the reign of the antichrist.

Revelation 3: 7 - 10 (NIV)

> 7. To the angel of the church in Philadelphia write: These are the words of him who is holy and true, who holds the key of David. What he opens no one can shut, and what he shuts no one can open.
> 8. I know your deeds. See, I have placed before you an open door that no one can shut. I know that you have little strength, yet you have kept my word and have not denied my name.
> 9. I will make those who are of the synagogue of Satan, who claim to be Jews though they are not, but are liars—I will make them come and fall down at your feet and acknowledge that I have loved you.
> 10. Since you have kept my command to endure patiently, I will also keep you from the hour of trial that is going to come on the whole world to test the inhabitants of the earth.

In 1 Thessalonians 4:17, believers are told that those who are still alive will be taken to meet Jesus in the air. This was discussed earlier in Chapter 10, The Time is Near. There is the possibility that not all believers will be taken to meet Jesus in the air. The parable of the ten virgins in Matthew 25, tells of five being ready and five not being ready.

Meeting Christ in the air is not discussed in the Book of Revelation. Many scholars and writers believe it will occur before the woes; and accordingly, this is why it is not mentioned in the Revelation. My reasoning for its inclusion at this point, is that after experiencing woes, many would be drawn closer to Jesus. But most importantly, God knows the timing and it will happen.

3. The Two Beasts and their Reign, (the last three and one-half years)

Revelation 13: 1-4 (NIV)

> 1.The dragon stood on the shore of the sea. And I saw a beast come out of the sea. It had ten horns and seven heads, with ten crowns on its horns, and on each head a blasphemous name.
> 2. The beast I saw resembled a leopard, but had feet like those of a bear and a mouth like that of a lion. The dragon gave the beast his power and his throne and great authority.
> 3. One of the heads of the beast seemed to have had a fatal wound, but the fatal wound had been healed. The whole world was filled with wonder and followed the beast.
> 4. People worshiped the dragon because he had given authority to the beast, and they also worshiped the beast and asked, "Who is like the beast? Who can wage war against it?"

In Revelation 13:1, the beast has ten horns, each with its own crown. This could signify that the beast is given authority to rule the nations of the world. Also in verse 1, we are told that the beast has seven heads, and on each head, a blasphemous name. The seven heads could imply a number of leaders, one of whom is singled out in Revelation 13:3 as having had a fatal wound, but the fatal wound had been healed.

So, who or what is the beast to whom Satan the dragon, gives his power in verse 2? It would be a power existing today that has come out of the fourth empire in Nebuchadnezzar's dream in Daniel 2. The beast would be the little horn that appears in Daniel 7:8 and 7:25 bringing the influence of the fourth empire to the world, the iron mixed with clay.

Revelation 13: 5 – 10 (NIV)

> 5. The beast was given a mouth to utter proud words and blasphemies and to exercise its authority for forty-two months.
> 6. It opened its mouth to blaspheme God, and to slander his name and his dwelling place and those who live in heaven.
> 7. It was given power to wage war against God's holy people and to conquer them. And it was given authority over every tribe, people, language and nation.
> 8. All inhabitants of the earth will worship the beast—all whose names have not been written in the Lamb's book of life, the Lamb who was slain from the creation of the world.
> 9. Whoever has ears, let them hear.
> 10. "If anyone is to go into captivity, into captivity they will go. If anyone is to be killed with the sword, with the sword they will be killed." This calls for patient endurance and faithfulness on the part of God's people.

These verses speak of a beast who has great power. He will wage war against God's people and say terrible things against God. All the inhabitants on earth who are not believers will willingly worship the beast.

We know from Daniel 7:25 and 9:27 that the beast will rule the world for three and one-half years. This period of time is equivalent to Revelation 13:5 which states that the beast will have authority for forty-two months.

Verse 10 is very sobering. Anyone who insists on staying true to God's Holy Word will have to hide or they will be killed.

Revelation 13: 11 – 18 (NIV)

> 11. Then I saw a second beast, coming out of the earth. It had two horns like a lamb, but it spoke like a dragon.

12. It exercised all the authority of the first beast on its behalf, and made the earth and its inhabitants worship the first beast, whose fatal wound had been healed.

13. And it performed great signs, even causing fire to come down from heaven to the earth in full view of the people.

14. Because of the signs it was given power to perform on behalf of the first beast, it deceived the inhabitants of the earth. It ordered them to set up an image in honor of the beast who was wounded by the sword and yet lived.

15. The second beast was given power to give breath to the image of the first beast, so that the image could speak and cause all who refused to worship the image to be killed.

16. It also forced all people, great and small, rich and poor, free and slave, to receive a mark on their right hands or on their foreheads,

17. so that they could not buy or sell unless they had the mark, which is the name of the beast or the number of its name.

18. This calls for wisdom. Let the person who has insight calculate the number of the beast, for it is the number of a man. That number is 666.

In verse 11, a second beast comes out of the earth; it is both like a lamb and a dragon. In verse 12, the head that had the fatal wound now becomes the first beast. The second beast makes all the inhabitants of the earth worship the first beast whose fatal wound had been healed. This may be difficult to understand but Revelation 13:12 singles out one of the seven heads to become the first beast. This is similar to Revelation 13:3 which singles out one of the heads: *"One of the heads of the beast seemed to have had a fatal wound, but the fatal wound had been healed."* The beast with seven heads referred to in Revelation 13:1 could be interpreted or seen as an entity with a number of leaders while the beast in Revelation 13:12 is one of the leaders who was wounded.

In verses 12 and 13, the second beast exercises all the power and authority of the first beast, the one with the healed fatal wound, and the second beast performs great signs that amazes many. In verse 14, the second beast orders people to build an image of the first beast. Why would there be an image? Where is this first beast, has he already died? Using a holographic image would fool people.

All must worship the image of the first beast, the one with the fatal wound that was healed.

In Revelation 13:15, the second beast gives breath to the first beast. The image is now alive and it yields its power to have many killed. This information tells us that the little horn of Daniel prophecy will have had a fatal wound but lived. We now know that the beast will have to fit this description. From Revelation 13, we also know there will be two leaders. One who is alive and very clever and deceitful, and the second, who starts off as an image but comes alive again.

Reflections on the End Times

At the end of the Book of Daniel, he is told to seal up his prophecies for the time is far off. I believe that the time has come to understand them. These prophecies of Daniel have laid the foundation for our understanding of the Revelation prophecies. To recount, the last kingdoms to be ruled by man are the ten toes of the statue of Nebuchadnezzar's dream. These toes would be the ten horns in Revelation 13:1. These are today's countries as seen through the eyes of God. The toes are made of clay but mixed with iron. The iron signifies the power and influence of the fourth empire. In Daniel's vision of the four beasts, it again gives us the fourth empire that had control of ten countries and among these countries a little horn comes up. Daniel 7:21 tells us the little horn becomes a power unto itself and speaks against God and wages war against the holy people. During the time of the little horn, a divine power intervenes and power is handed over to God. I believe this little horn is the beast in Revelation 13. And the divine power that intervenes is Jesus Christ.

Our current world order is at risk especially with the accumulated debt that most nations are experiencing. This could easily lead to civil unrest that would be overwhelming and provide the impetus for nations to come together. Finding solutions for a world in crisis both economically and socially, would be paramount.

This would give a charismatic leader an opportunity to come forward to help restore order and end suffering. Nations would arrange an agreement for his service. Most countries of the world would be signatories. This would occur during the first year of the last period of one 'sevens'.

In the middle of the seven years, the charismatic leader with only a few people will come to Jerusalem and rule from there. Many believe that Israel will rebuild the temple before or during the end times. However, I suggest as an alternate scenario that the leader will move to Jerusalem and rule from the existing structure at the temple mount.

Daniel 9: 27 (NIV)

> 27. He will confirm a covenant with many for one 'seven.' In the middle of the 'seven' he will put an end to sacrifice and offering. And at the temple he will set up an abomination that causes desolation, until the end that is decreed is poured out on him.

During the last half of the seven years, Revelation 13:14 says that the leader, who is referred to as the second beast, will order people to set up an image of a former leader (called the first beast) who was intentionally wounded during his life but lived, but who is now dead. This image will be set up on the current temple mount. The leader will also not allow the Jews to continue with their "sacrifice and offering," the daily prayers that are constantly being said at the Western Wall. The setting up of the image, and the stopping of the sacrifice and offering are referred to in Daniel 9:27 as the "abomination that causes desolation."

This leader, the second beast will give breath to the image and the person will come alive. Together, they will reign for three and one-half years from Jerusalem. Terror will be excessive. This will culminate in many nations joining themselves together. They come to a place called

Armageddon ready for war against God's people. Their end will come with Jesus Christ winning the battle for God's people. I believe that the unfolding of these end time events could be in our near future.

4. The Fall of Babylon, (a point in time)

Many years ago, Daniel, the Hebrew, was captured and taken to Babylonia. He was asked to interpret King Nebuchadnezzar's dream. The dream was of a large statue and had a head of gold. Daniel told the King the gold head was the kingdom of Babylon. He also told the king, Babylon stood by itself in greatness. The remainder of the statue were future kingdoms but all inferior to Babylon.

Here we are again, at another point in time with another Babylon. We are told that the whole world will come under the control of the beast. Accordingly, this will likely be the fall of the world's economic system. Many people have always put their hope for wealth and security in an economic system built on rules of men. We might want to re-evaluate this trend. Where will this lead us and is it sustainable, especially when we are all in debt, which is quickly getting worse due to the world responding to the Covid-19 pandemic.

This Babylon comes under the judgement of God. The merchants of the earth lament, for in one day, plagues and fires consume her. In the throne room of God, there comes a threefold hallelujah. "Hallelujah! Salvation and glory and power belong to our God for true and just are his judgements." (Revelation 19:1)

5. The Second Coming of Jesus Christ, (a point in time)

We are told in Matthew 24:30, *"Then will appear the sign of the Son of Man in Heaven. And then all the peoples of the earth will mourn when they see the Son of Man coming on the clouds of heaven, with power and great glory."* Everyone will see Jesus Christ when he comes to earth. All will be astonished. This will be the greatest event ever in terms of its impact on the future of people. Finally, the world will come under the leadership of a righteous ruler, Jesus Christ. Ever since Adam and Eve were removed from the garden of Eden, the earth has been ruled by men, leading to conflict and suffering for most. For the last two thousand years people have been expecting Jesus to return to earth and then it will have happened.

It will not be necessary to ask people if we are there yet for the second coming of Jesus Christ. We will know the time is right from our past experiences. Those whose names were written in the Lamb's Book of Life will have already met Jesus in the air. The remainder who are alive, will have experienced the woes as well as the reign of the three and one-half years of the beast.

Many will have repented during the woes. In Revelation 7:9, we are told that many will show up in the throne room of God who came out of the tribulation period. They are dressed in white; this indicates that their sins have been forgiven through their belief in Jesus. They are from every nation and tribe, and they are so numerous they cannot be counted.

In Revelation 14:1, Jesus is standing on Mount Zion with 144, 000. These are the Jewish people who were sealed in Revelation 7:4, and who now stand with Jesus. An interesting statement on these are given in Revelation 14:4, "they have not defiled themselves with woman (sin)". Since all sin, the only explanation for this is they now have accepted Jesus as Savior, and have been cleansed by his blood.

Revelation 19: 11 -16 (NIV)

> 11. I saw heaven standing open and there before me was a white horse, whose rider is called Faithful and True. With justice he judges and wages war.
> 12. His eyes are like blazing fire, and on his head are many crowns. He has a name written on him that no one knows but he himself.
> 13. He is dressed in a robe dipped in blood, and his name is the Word of God.

> 14. The armies of heaven were following him, riding on white horses and dressed in fine linen, white and clean.
> 15. Coming out of his mouth is a sharp sword with which to strike down the nations. "He will rule them with an iron scepter." He treads the winepress of the fury of the wrath of God Almighty.
> 16. On his robe and on his thigh, he has this name written: King of Kings and Lord of Lords.

These Scriptures give a description of Jesus coming to earth. He comes as a warrior ready for battle with a sharp sword in his mouth, his robe is dipped in blood, which is a stark reminder of his cruel death. The sharp sword is a powerful image. Could it be God's Word? In Hebrew 4:12, we are told that the Word of God is alive and active, sharper than any double-edged sword, and in John 1:1, we are told that Jesus is the Word of God. He does not need a bomb, a machine gun or any physical weapon of war. He will likely use his words to accomplish his purposes. God spoke and made the universe; divine words are powerful. Many come with Jesus, riding on white horses dressed in white. They can dress in white because they will not need to fight a battle, Jesus will speak and the battle will be won.

Hebrews 4: 12 (NIV)

> 12. For the word of God is alive and active. Sharper than any double-edged sword, it penetrates even to dividing soul and spirit, joints and marrow; it judges the thoughts and attitudes of the heart.

All nations are willing to go to war against God's people. They come together at Armageddon. Many soldiers from all nations, including many who have crossed the Euphrates river, come prepared for battle. We are told that the earth would have been destroyed if Jesus Christ hadn't intervened.

In Revelation 19:20,21, the beast and the false prophet (the first and second beast) are captured. They are thrown alive into the fiery lake of burning sulfur. The rest are killed with the sword coming out of the mouth of Jesus. The streets run with their blood and angels call birds to come and eat their bodies. The final victory belongs to Jesus.

Ezekiel 39: 4, 7, 8 (NIV)

> 4. On the mountains of Israel you will fall, you and all your troops and the nations with you. I will give you as food to all kinds of carrion birds and to the wild animals.
> 7. I will make known my holy name among my people Israel. I will no longer let my holy name be profaned, and the nations will know that I the Lord am the Holy One in Israel.
> 8. It is coming! It will surely take place, declares the Sovereign LORD. This is the day I have spoken of.

6. The Reign of Jesus Christ on Earth, (one thousand years)

When Jesus sets up his reign, Earth is still with us. It was not destroyed by climate change or nuclear war. We as a people deserve no credit for our planet still remaining because the planet belongs to God. Nor was it destroyed by the massive earthquake in Revelation 16. I can only assume that if our atmosphere requires fixing, God the creator will know how to fix it.

Jesus Christ will become the King of all nations. Satan at this time, throughout Jesus' reign, will be locked in the abyss. He will no longer be an influence in people's lives. The Bible tells us that Jesus will rule with an iron scepter, or with a rod of iron. This likely means that humans continue to need stern laws. This thousand years on earth will be a time of great peace and safety, but we are not in our eternal home, that will come later.

In Revelation 20:4, we are told those who are martyred for their faith will come to earth and rule with Jesus. The Bible tells us that all who have been faithful upon Earth and have their names written in the Lamb's Book of Life, will also be with him. Will I be with Christ on Earth during his reign? I believe I will. (See 1 Thessalonians 4:17, and 5:10).

The Twelve Tribes of Israel

The Book of Ezekiel, Chapter 37, has the twelve tribes of Israel coming together again in Israel. I believe this will be with Jesus Christ during his thousand-year reign on Earth. Where did they come from and why?

It began by God calling a man called Abram. God changed his name to Abraham and sent him to a far away land, which became known as their promised land. He had two sons, Ishmael and Isaac. His second son Isaac, was the son of promise. Isaac had twin sons. The blessing of God was on the younger, named Jacob. God changed Jacob's name to Israel.

Israel had twelve sons who became the twelve tribes of Israel. They became the Chosen People of God, through whom God would reveal himself to all others. Overtime, the twelve tribes separated into two nation groups. Ten of the tribes became the Northern kingdom of Israel and two tribes became the kingdom of Judah. Through wars the kingdom of Israel became scattered. These became the lost tribes of Israel. The tribes of Judah and Benjamin became the kingdom of Judah. After many years the Babylonians captured Judah. The Jews did return and rebuilt the temple and the wall, however, others ruled over them. These Jews over time also became scattered all over the world. In 1948, after the Second World War, the nation state of Israel became a reality. They received permission for them to again have their promised land.

Ezekiel's Prophecies

Going back to Ezekiel's prophecies, aspects arise on the rule of Jesus Christ on earth. This book, written at the time when the nation of Israel no longer existed by Ezekiel ben-Buzi, gives amazing details. He was a priest living in exile in the city of Babylon between 593 and 571 BC. The Glory of the

Lord falls upon him. God calls Ezekiel to go to the Israelites and speak to them.

The Book of Ezekiel pronounces judgment on both Israel and surrounding nations. It also includes a prophecy of the resurrected twelve tribes of Israel. Ezekiel 37 presents a picture of the resurrection and restoration of God's people in a future kingdom. Ezekiel 40 – 48, give readers a picture of the reconstructed temple in Jerusalem, complete with the return of God's glory to His dwelling place. It describes clearly set out boundaries for each of the twelve tribes as well as a section for the temple of the King. I believe this is the millennial kingdom of Jesus Christ.

The Israelites, at the time when Ezekiel wrote this prophecy, were from the southern kingdom of Judah, mainly originating from two tribes, Benjamin, and Judah. However, under the reign of Jesus, the twelve tribes will be all together again.

The Loss of Nationhood

God's judgement came upon the southern kingdom because they spiritually moved away from God and instead of being an example, followed the idolatry of other nations. God spoke to them through prophets, especially Jeremiah. A specific prophecy was given to them by Jeremiah in Jerusalem just prior to the Babylonian invasion and then repeated via a letter from Jerusalem to the captives in Babylon. This prophecy foretold that the "land shall be a desolation" and that the Jews would "serve the king of Babylon seventy years" (Jeremiah 25:11, 29:10).

After seventy years, many Jews did return to their original homeland. Under the leadership of Ezra and Nehemiah, both the temple and the wall were rebuilt. However, they came under Persian rule. Their promised land had other conquerors: The Greek – Alexander the Great, followed by his generals, then followed by the Romans. Many years later in 1948, Israel again became a nation.

Renewing the Abrahamic Kingdom (Israel)

Why would God want to bring all twelve tribes back together? God tells us the renewing of the Abrahamic Kingdom is not necessarily for the benefit of Israel. He very much wants all people to know that He is God. When he says something, he will always accomplish what he promises. Re-establishing the complete nation of Israel was his promise to his people. He is a Holy God.

Ezekiel 36:22 (NIV)

> 22. Therefore say to the Israelites, "This is what the Sovereign Lord says: It is not for your sake, people of Israel, that I am going to do these things, but for the sake of my holy name, which you have profaned among the nations where you have gone."

Zephaniah 3:20 (NIV)

> 20. "At that time I will gather you; at that time I will bring you home. I will give you honor and praise among all the peoples of the earth when I restore your fortunes before your very eyes," says the Lord.

Isaiah 49: 8, 9 (NIV)

> 8.This is what the Lord says: "In the time of my favor I will answer you, and in the day of salvation I will help you; I will keep you and will make you to be a covenant for the people, to restore the land and to reassign its desolate inheritances,
> 9.to say to the captives, "Come out," and to those in darkness, "Be free!"

In Revelation 7, a direction is given not to harm the twelve tribes of Israel until 12,000 from each of the twelve tribes of Israel, are sealed. These 144,000 people will be resurrected and brought back to rule with Jesus.

The Messiah's Kingdom

The Messiah will set up his kingdom upon this earth as told in Revelation 20. This will also include the renewed Abrahamic Kingdom. When Jesus came as a babe in Bethlehem, many Jewish people would have known the location and this met their expectations. Also prophesied was that the Messiah would become a king and rule their kingdom. They must have been rather confused and disappointed when He returned to Heaven. What they did not understand was the timing.

Revelation 20 clearly tells us that Jesus Christ will set up his kingdom upon this earth, and this kingdom will last for a thousand years. Not only will he set up his kingdom, the twelve tribes of Israel will rule and reign with him as well as all believers.

7. Satan's Return and the Last Falling Away, (for a short time)

Revelation 20:7 – 10 (NIV)

> 7. When the thousand years are over, Satan will be released from his prison
> 8. and will go out to deceive the nations in the four corners of the earth—Gog and Magog—and to gather them for battle. In number they are like the sand on the seashore.
> 9. They marched across the breadth of the earth and surrounded the camp of God's people, the city he loves. But fire came down from heaven and devoured them.
> 10. And the devil, who deceived them, was thrown into the lake of burning sulfur, where the beast and the false prophet had been thrown. They will be tormented day and night for ever and ever."

The above Scripture are rather surprising. Satan was locked in the abyss during the thousand years of Jesus' reign. People came under Jesus' leadership and experienced his goodness. One would think that Satan's lies would not affect them. However, this is not what happens, people again join Satan. They come from all over the earth and surrounded "the camp of God's people." this probably refers to the area given to the twelve tribes of Israel in Ezekiel 47:13 – 34, including Jerusalem. They are so numerous they are like the sand of the seashore. Again, Jesus responds quickly with awesome power. Fire comes down from Heaven and destroys them. In conclusion, we see that Jesus again is victorious. Like it or not, people are no match for the divine.

8. The Judgement of the Dead, (a point in time)

Writing about this judgement is very difficult because I connect with people in a deep and real way. We are all very complex individuals who are shaped by our DNA, our families, cultures, traditions, and circumstances, and no one asked to be born. Over my lifetime, I have met many people and each person is amazingly complex and each one is inherently beautiful.

It breaks my heart reading Revelation 20:11 – 15 that those who haven't accepted Jesus will be judged and set apart from God forever. Books will be opened as the dead both great and small stand before God. We are told that the Book of Life will be there as well as other books. Each will see that their name is not in the Book of Life because they did not believe in God, even though they saw and experienced his goodness through his creation nor did they realize their need for a Savior.

What will be the outcome of people who died in their sin? The Bible tells us they will be judged by what they did in their lives. What people do with their lives does matter to God, and should matter to individuals as they will have to stand before God. It appears that there will be eternal separation from God with differing degrees of punishment. In 2 Peter 3: 8, 9 it appears that unbelievers will perish (a forever death).

Judgement of the Believers

To finalize the topic on Judgement, I ask the question, what about those whose sins have been forgiven by Jesus Christ? People, who are believers will be judged at a different time by Jesus. Believers will stand before the judgement seat of Christ and give an account of themselves. They too will be judged for what they did with their time on Earth. See Romans 14:10 –12, and also 2 Corinthians 5:10. A believer's work will be judged but not their sins because sins have already been judged and paid for by Jesus Christ. However, believers should do work that pleases Jesus. In I Corinthians 3:11 – 15, we are told that work undertaken based on our wrong desires will be burned, though the believer will be saved. The judgement of a believer's works will occur when they meet Jesus in the air (1 Thessalonians 4:16 – 18).

God's Ultimate Purpose

Remember, that God has an ultimate purpose. What is this purpose? I believe this purpose is why the whole universe along with this Earth was created in the first place. It takes us back to the beginning. God made humanity special, in his image. He made intelligent human beings who are capable of thinking and making choices. Would any willingly choose to acknowledge him? We are told that God reveals his power and knowledge to us through everything he has created so none have an excuse. From reading the Bible and personal experience, I will say many will accept their salvation, but unfortunately many have chosen not to follow a Holy God, or perhaps not had the opportunity. Here is where the ministry of planting and sowing comes in. All believers should be co-workers with God. Those who were able to humble themselves and have their robes washed white through their belief in Christ Jesus will become the Bride of Jesus Christ.

9. The End of Time as We Know It, (a point in time)

I don't think there has ever been a person who has experienced living on earth who has not marveled at all that we have. It all works together; one element supports another and so on. Every element is important and exceedingly complex. We need the sun, the atmosphere, the soil, the rain, the dry land and sea. The life on our earth, from the smallest to the biggest is amazing. And all this works with the concept of time.

Revelation 21: 1 (NIV)

> 1. Then I saw a new heaven and a new earth, for the first heaven and the first earth had passed away, and there was no longer any sea.

Everyone wants to prevent the destruction of Earth. We would like Earth to continue for ever and ever. God in his wisdom, has another plan. The end of time and the destruction of all that we now have, will happen.

10. A New Place Appears – New Jerusalem, (for eternity)

Revelation 22:3 – 5 (NIV)

> 3. No longer will there be any curse. The throne of God and of the Lamb will be in the city, and his servants will serve him.
> 4. They will see his face, and his name will be on their foreheads.
> 5. There will be no more night. They will not need the light of a lamp or the light of the sun, for the Lord God will give them light. And they will reign for ever and ever.

The God of power and knowledge created everything we now have, and again he will be giving us a new beginning. A new home for the Bride of Jesus Christ. God, our Heavenly Father and our Lord and Savior, Jesus Christ will be on the throne. There is no longer the need for the sun. The concept of time and the physical universe are gone. These marvellous creations by God have served his purposes. In Revelation 22, a new reality is introduced, our new home, New Jerusalem. God, himself is there. He and our Lord Jesus Christ will be its light. God's people will be with him, the Bride of Christ, those whose names are written in the Lamb's Book of Life. The reality of eternal life will begin for those who have submitted their lives to Jesus Christ. In this new reality there will be no need for laws to live by. There will be no illnesses or tears or emotional pain. God's peace and love will reign supreme.

The Book of Revelation sets out the dimensions of New Jerusalem. It is laid out as a square, with thick walls. It has a river flowing through the city that comes from the throne room of God. There are trees on the sides of the river. The trees produce fruit for the healing of the nations. This likely speaks of people from the different nations of the world. There appears to be animals. In Isaiah 11:6, all animals live together in peace and harmony.

> 6. The wolf will live with the lamb, the leopard will lie down with the goat, the calf and the lion and the yearling together; and a little child will lead them.

We will be given our roles in our new home based on what we did with our earthly time. Being ushered into New Jerusalem to reside with our Heavenly Father and our Savior, Jesus Christ, finally happens. And if we can think about our past struggles, they will be as nothing. So today we know what is ahead. With eternity as our focus, we can submit each day of our lives to God, and soldier on. My prayer is that people on God's Earth will choose to follow Jesus. We will then all come together as the Bride of Jesus Christ.

Chapter 15

Claim Your Inheritance

Our Lives Today

Living on earth can be both difficult and joyful. We often face sickness, disappointments, and hardships and some that we cannot even imagine. So why in the world are we here? While we have times of joy, there is also pain and despair. What are our lives all about?

Many live without answers doing their best to survive. Usually, survival is in the context of having to do better or at least keeping up with one's neighbour. And if the truth be known, the saying that birds of a feather flock together, propel us to identify with the flock we are in. We treasure it mainly because this comes as a birthright. The tribe in which we are born.

Learning Truths

Writing this book gave me the opportunity to ponder many important truths. I have the knowledge of what is before me, and this allows me to realize that God has a plan and I am part of that plan. I am joyful realizing that everyone is important to God, and he wants all people to be part of his plan. As such, I conclude this book by talking about an inheritance. I believe each person has the right to a special inheritance from God.

The things I have written about in this discourse, I believe to be true, and events will unfold as prophesied in the Bible. God wants all to know these things but most importantly, he wants us to know and stand on our inheritance. So, what is this inheritance that awaits us? Do we just die and that is the end? Without the knowledge of God, our current lives would be all that we have, so I understand how that shapes our thinking. We seek to make the most of life daily, for ourselves, our family and those around us.

With a knowledge of God our minds can begin to shift to something different, something bigger. When we consider the concept that there might not be an end, our thinking is challenged. The thought of an all-powerful, eternal God who created everything, including us, makes us think there might be a future. We now ask the question, where do I fit in. God, the creator of the universe, would he want to bother with me? The answer is a definite yes.

God wants all to know he is always with us. He is powerful and merciful and wants each of us, from the weakest to the strongest, to become aware of him. He also wants us to know how much we are loved by him. Your past does not matter. Your race does not matter, your education does not matter. How rich or poor you are, does not matter. What matters is your knowledge and trust of God.

He has a love for each and everyone that cannot be measured. We are more precious than gold or anything we would deem valuable. God loves us all, and we are all equal. There is an eternal inheritance waiting for you and for me and He wants all to claim this precious gift.

Our Inheritance

Our inheritance is something for us to obtain not only for the future but also for the present, and as said earlier, it is more precious that gold. We become children of God Almighty. This is our inheritance for today and for an eternity.

This is a gift to all who believe in Christ Jesus. Jesus has paid our sin debt. Belief in his goodness activated through repentance of our sins, reconciles us back to the Almighty God, our Heavenly Father. There is absolutely no other way back to the Father. Once we do this, everything changes. Our promised inheritance is no longer a promise but a profound truth living within us. We can live every day in a new sphere of God's grace and power. We begin to see ourselves and others differently. We also become aware of the many promises of God that are part of our inheritance. Reading the Holy Bible, and attending a Bible believing church, will educate us of his power and promises. A rewarding experience will be ours as we embrace our new reality. We are now children of God Almighty. No longer are we mere humans tossed about by every storm of life.

The best answer to the question "Are We There Yet," is to arrive at this truth; knowing your value and importance to God and knowing how much you are loved by our Lord Jesus Christ. God wants to impart his wisdom to us, give us our daily provisions, help us in troubled times, and bring us into his will and calling on our lives.

This is all ours simply through belief. The very best news of all, our names will be written in the Lamb's Book of Life, which gives us eternal life. We can stand strong as we claim our inheritance. Use it today, use it tomorrow and everyday as we move forward and live out our lives on Earth and beyond.

This inheritance is what God the Father wants for his beloved creation. He wants all to accept His Son, Jesus as our Savior and be reconciled back to himself. To everyone I say, do look at today as an opportunity to claim your inheritance. Should you already be a Christian, a believer in Jesus

Christ, today is a day to strengthen your resolve to claim your inheritance and take your stand. Nothing can take away the love that Jesus Christ has for us.

Soon and very soon we will be with Him. Soon and very soon we will be the Bride of Christ and live with our Heavenly Father and Jesus Christ in New Jerusalem. Come, Lord Jesus, come. Amen.

Endnotes

Sources of Information

1. Information on World War Two:
   https://www.history.com/topics/world-war-ii
2. Information on the United Nations: https://www.un.org
3. Information on Nato: https://www.nato.int
4. Information on the European Union:
   https://europa.eu/european-union
5. Information on Populations:
   https://www.livepopulation.com/population-projections/
6. Information on Poverty: https://data.worldbank.org
7. Information on Daniel 9:
   https://enduringword.com/bible-commentary/daniel-9

Annex A

Four Prophecies of Daniel (Page 1 of 2)

THE PROPHECY:	END TIMES INFORMATION:	THE FINAL END TIMES OUTCOME:
1. King Nebuchadnezzar's Dream: Daniel 2: A Large Statue that represents all empires of the world starting with Babylon. The fourth kingdom would be the Roman Empire. It is of iron. It is strong and fierce and crushes others. The statue ends with two feet and ten toes.	The ten toes would represent present day nations, including the end times. The two feet and ten toes are made partly of iron and partly of clay. Signifying that the power and influence of Rome continues today in nations.	Daniel 2: 44 (NIV) 44: In the time of those kings (ten toes) the God of heaven will set up a kingdom that will never be destroyed, nor will it be left to another people. It (God's kingdom) will crush all these kingdoms and bring them to an end, but it will itself endure forever.
2. Daniel's Dream of Four Beasts Daniel 7: A lion, a bear, and a leopard. The fourth beast does not have a name. The four beasts again represent the same empires as in Nebuchadnezzar's dream. The fourth beast would be the Roman Empire. It is terrifying and frightening. It has ten horns and among the horns, a little horn appears. The little horn has a mouth and speaks boastfully against God.	Daniel 7: 25 25: He will speak against the Most High and oppress his holy people and try to change the set times and the laws. The holy people will be delivered into his hands for a time, times, and half a time. (time = 1 year) (Times = 2 years) Therefore, this little horn will rule the holy people for three and one-half years. This is the same amount of time given in months for the rule of the beast in Revelation 13:5.	Daniel 7:26, 27 26: But the court will sit, and the power will be taken away from him, and completely destroyed forever. 27: Then the sovereignty, power and greatness of all the kingdoms under heaven will be handed over to the holy people of the Most High. His kingdom will be an everlasting kingdom.

THE PROPHECY:	END TIMES INFORMATION:	THE FINAL END TIMES OUTCOME:
3. Seventy "Sevens" Daniel 9:20-27 Gabriel, an angel tells Daniel there will be seventy 'sevens' (490 years) before God establishes His kingdom on Earth. The first 483 years have been fulfilled. From the time of the chosen people returning to Jerusalem to rebuild the city to when Jesus rode into Jerusalem one week before his death was 483 years. See Endnote 7 for further explanation on the seventy 'sevens.'	The last one sevens remain yet to be fulfilled. The one seven means seven years. These would be the years of the end times, basically the last seven years of man's reign on earth. 2000 plus years have occurred between the 483 years and the last seven which is yet to be fulfilled. This is the time on earth when people can accept their Savior, Jesus Christ.	Daniel 9:27: 27: He (the beast or anti-christ) will confirm a covenant with many for one seven. In the middle of the seven, he will put an end to sacrifice an offering. And at the temple, he will set up an abomination that causes desolation, until the end that is decreed is poured out on him.
4. The King of the South and the King of the North Struggles between the two kings occur, culminating in the events of the last seven years of the end times.	Daniel 11 &12 The king of the North will gain favor through intrigue. He will set up his kingdom in Jerusalem and do as he please. He will speak against the true God in Heaven. He comes with a few people but many will follow him. It will be a terrible time upon the earth.	Daniel 11:45 "…Yet he will come to his end, and no one will help him. At a time decreed by God, the evil King will be destroyed. God will set up a kingdom that will never end." This is the same kingdom spoken of in all four prophecies. The reign of earth moves from man to God.

Annex B

Summary of the Book of Revelation

Revelation 1, 2, 3, 4, 5, 6, 7	Messages to seven churches. Seven seals are opened. The first four seals: horses, an overview of powers on Earth. The 5th seal: those who have been martyred cry out for Justice, The 6th Seal: a major earthquake, this earthquake appears to be the one that occurs just after Jesus's second coming (see Revelation, Chapter 16:18). Also under the 6th Seal,144,000 people from the twelve tribes of Israel are sealed so they are not harmed. And again, under the same seal, multitudes show up in heaven, these are those who came out of the great tribulation. The 7th Seal reveals seven angels with seven trumpets.
Revelation 8, 9	The Woes – Seven angels sound seven trumpets. These woes cause harm to one third of Earth. Hail and fire, a huge mountain falls into the sea, and a third of the sun, moon and stars become dark. A volcano, and locusts and scorpions. These appear to be weapons.
Revelation 10, 11, 12	In Chapter 10, John eats a little scroll. It ends with him saying that he must prophesy again to many peoples, nations, languages and kings. In addition, God sends two witnesses to prophesy for 1,260 days (the time of the Beast's reign). They are killed but come back to life. All people of Earth will see them. Probably through the use of the internet.
Revelation 12	What woman could this be? Probably believers in Christ. She will be protected for the 1260 days, (three and one-half years) again, the number of days the Beast/antichrist will have power upon the earth. The chapter goes on to tell the story about Satan. He is thrown out of heaven to the earth and one third of the angels followed him. It finishes by saying that Satan went off to wage war against God's people and those who believe in Jesus. A dire warning here.

Revelation 13	A beast comes out of the sea (an institution) and a second beast comes out of the earth (a leader). The Beast blasphemes God and is given authority over all nations. The second beast sets up an image of a former leader who has died (This image leader and is now called the first beast). All who refuse to worship the image are killed. The image is given breath (life) and together they rule. They rule from Jerusalem for 42 months (the three and one-half years period as given in Daniel). Also, only those who have mark of the beast or his number 666, will be allowed to buy and sell.
Revelation 14, 15,16	John sees the Lamb, standing on Mount Zion and with him are the 144,000 from the twelve tribes of Israel. Three angels appear. The first angel has the eternal gospel. The second tells all that Babylon has fallen, and the third, pronounces God's fury on anyone who worshipped the Beast. Following this all people living on earth are harvested. In Chapters 15 and 16, seven angels with the seven last plagues appear. Seven bowls of wrath are poured out on Earth. These happen to people who have accepted the mark of the beast: 1. Festering sores on people. 2. The sea turns to blood and everything in the sea dies. 3. All rivers and springs of water turn to blood. 4. the sun scorches people with intense heat. 5. Wrath is poured out on the beast. People have pain and sores. Yet, they refuse to repent. It appears that these woes are a last attempt by God to bring people to himself. 6. When the six angel pours, the great river Euphrates, dries up to make way for the kings of the East.
	Also, from the sixth bowl, three impure Spirits come, from the dragon, beast, and false prophet. They perform signs, and they convince all the kings of the world to come together for the battle on the great day of God Almighty. In Chapter 16, verse 15, Jesus Christ "comes as a thief in the night." In verse 16, the kings come together at Armageddon. In verses 17 and 18, the 7th angel pours out his bowl, a severe earthquake occurs and the cites of the nations collapse. No earthquake like it has ever occurred since mankind has been on Earth.

Revelation 17, 18, 19	The fall of Babylon. She has become a fallen place for demons. A voice from heaven asks people to come out of Babylon. Instead the wicked weep for Babylon. Babylon's doom: The city will be thrown down," by your magic spells all nations were led astray". Threefold Hallelujah over Babylon's Fall comes from Heaven. She had fine white linen but it was rejected. Babylon could be the world's economic system. In Chapter 19:11 Jesus faces the kings of the earth who come to Armageddon to attack God's people. Jesus comes as a warrior and he has victory. Birds are called to come and eat the flesh of the many who came to attack. The two beasts are thrown in a lake of burning sulfur.
Revelation 20, 21, 22	20. The thousand years reign of Christ, the judgement of the dead. 21. New heaven and earth, new Jerusalem. 22. Eden restored, invitation and warning.

CPSIA information can be obtained
at www.ICGtesting.com
Printed in the USA
BVHW071250190720
583905BV00001B/49